NEW WINE AND OLD BOTTLES

Notre Dame Studies on International Peace

Joan B. Kroc Institute for International Peace Studies
University of Notre Dame

With the end of the Cold War the promise and relevance of peace research have significantly increased. The issues now addressed include the nature of the world order, international institutions, the resolution of deadly conflicts, humanitarian security, and ethical issues raised by violence, environmental degradation, and poverty. Peace studies probe these problems and search for comprehensive solutions.

Notre Dame Studies on International Peace focuses on these vital issues. Scholarly perspectives are combined with sound policy recommendations and the setting of normative standards. The books published here emanate primarily from the research work of the Kroc Institute and its other activities, especially the annual Theodore M. Hesburgh, C.S.C., Lectures on Ethics and Public Policy.

These lectures were launched in 1995 by the Joan B. Kroc Institute for International Peace Studies to honor the lifetime commitment of the President Emeritus of the University of Notre Dame to the promotion of ethical values in public policy and his continung support of the Institute. *New Wine and Old Bottles: International Politics and Ethical Discourse* results from the lectures in 1996 delivered by Professor Jean Bethke Elshtain of the University of Chicago.

Previously published in the series *Notre Dame Studies on International Peace* are *India and the Bomb: Public Opinion and Nuclear Options,* edited by David Cortright and Amitabh Mattoo, and *The Ethics and Politics of Humanitarian Intervention,* by Stanley Hoffmann (the 1995 Hesburgh Lectures).

Joan B. Kroc Institute for International Peace Studies was established at the University of Notre Dame in 1986. In addition to research projects, the Institute has an international graduate program and an undergraduate concentration in peace studies. It is a premier institute in its field in the United States. More information can be obtained from the Kroc Institute, P.O. Box 639, University of Notre Dame, Notre Dame, IN 46556, USA (phone 219-631-6970, fax 219-631-6973).

NEW WINE
AND
OLD BOTTLES

International Politics
and Ethical Discourse

Jean Bethke Elshtain

With contributions by Fred Dallmayr,
Martha Merritt, and Raimo Väyrynen

University of Notre Dame Press

Notre Dame, Indiana

Copyright 1998 by
University of Notre Dame Press
Notre Dame, Indiana 46556
All Rights Reserved
Manufactured in the United States of America

Library of Congress Cataloging-in-Publication Data

Elshtain, Jean Bethke, 1941–
    New wine and old bottles : international politics and ethical
discourse / Jean Bethke Elshtain ; with contributions by Fred R.
Dallmayr, Martha Merritt, and Raimo Väyrynen.
        p.   cm.—(Notre Dame Studies on International Peace)
    Includes bibliographical references.
    ISBN 0–268–01483–3 (pbk. : alk. paper)
    1. International relations—Moral and ethical aspects.   I. Title.
JZ1306.E44   1998   97–49698
174'.4—dc21

The paper used in this publication meets the minimum requirements
of the American National Standard for Information Sciences—
Permanence of Paper for Printed Library Materials, ANSI Z39.48-1984.

To democratic citizens who live in hope

CONTENTS

CONTRIBUTORS

Jean Bethke Elshtain is the Laura Spelman Rockefeller Professor of Social and Political Ethics at the University of Chicago Divinity School, a Fellow of the American Academy of Arts and Sciences, and a former Guggenheim Fellow. Her recent books include *Democracy on Trial* (1995), *Augustine and the Limits of Politics* (1995), and *Real Politics: At the Center of Everyday Life* (1997).

Fred Dallmayr is the Packey J. Dee Professor of Government and International Studies and a fellow of the Joan B. Kroc Institute for International Peace Studies at the University of Notre Dame. His main field is political philosophy, with a focus on contemporary political theory and cross-cultural hermeneutics. Among his recent books are *Hegel: Modernity and Politics* (1993), *The Other Heidegger* (1993), *Beyond Orientalism: Essays on Cross-Cultural Encounter* (1996), and *Alternative Visions: Paths in the Global Village* (1997).

Martha Merritt is Assistant Professor in the Department of Government and International Studies and a fellow of the Joan B. Kroc Institute for International Peace Studies at the University of Notre Dame. She is writing a book on the politics of nation in Estonia. Her most recent publication is "Contemplating Collapse and 'Democracy' in Russia," *Review of Politics*, Spring 1997.

Raimo Väyrynen is Professor of Government and International Studies and John M. Regan, Jr. Director of the Joan B. Kroc Institute for International Peace Studies at the University of Notre Dame. His research interests are in conflict and security studies, and theory and history of international relations. His most recent books are *Military Industrialization and Economic Development* (1992), a biography of Urho Kekkonen (1994), and *Global Transformation: Economics, Politics, and Culture* (1997).

Foreword

SOVEREIGNTY AND NATIONALISM IN A NEW KEY

Raimo Väyrynen

THE PRINCIPLE OF sovereignty has ordered international life for
the last 350 years, after the Peace of Westphalia brought an end
to 150 years of continuous fighting in Europe. This peace created
an international system based on the norm and practice of exclusion;
rulers were denied the right to impose any particular political and
religious order on the territories of other rulers. In that sense, sovereignty was constructed to preserve peace between political units
by separating the advocates of rivaling values and policies from each
other and confining them to their own territories. Thus, the "modern" international order was based on the exclusive territorial and
political division of the "civilized" world into emerging states.

The relationship between sovereignty and peace, however, has
also another aspect. Initially, sovereignty was intended to regulate
not only relations between states but also, perhaps even more fundamentally, their internal conditions, characterized by lawlessness
and violence. The establishment of the sovereign state as a supreme
coercive authority was intended to alter these conditions.

In the words of Tamaž Mastnak: "The invention of state . . . was
a response to the social violence ravaging late medieval and early
modern Europe. The state was conceived and instituted in order to
put an end to that violence by disarming society, and monopolizing
and legalizing the means and the use of violence".[1] Thus, the new
international system of states was not based, either externally or internally, on genuine tolerance and respect for differences, but rather

xi

was an instrumental arrangement to keep violence within and between entities in check. Such an arrangement did not emerge peace-
fully, however, but required large-scale use of violence by which the
emerging state defeated rivaling political organizations.[2] The new
international order was violently created.

The practice of sovereignty permitted the relatively peaceful co-
existence of states but did not create a transnational community,
since sovereignty, in the end, was grounded in the principles of distance and difference. Sovereignty also contains seeds of arrogance,
which sprouted especially after its association with nationalism became explicit in the nineteenth century. Sovereignty was considered
a fixed legal and territorial principle which fostered intolerance; it
underpinned the growing tendency to judge other people unfavor-
ably on the basis of what they were rather than what they did.[3]

In particular, in the twentieth century, the divided political order
of the world was unable to maintain peace, and the territorial state
often was used as a springboard of aggression against other states.
The standard realist argument stresses that the wars of this century
are due to the breakdown of the balance of power, to aggression,
and to appeasement. However, one should not underestimate the
extent to which these wars have been fueled by political intolerance
and the exclusive definition of self-determination.

This historical assessment of sovereignty does not give much reason to celebrate it, but rather encourages us to seek alternatives to it.
However, before debunking sovereignty in its entirety, one should
look at its other, less grim sides. Historically, it seems obvious that
the principle of sovereignty has pacified international relations. It
has provided arguments for the weak states to protect themselves
against the strong and helped great powers to maintain stability
in their mutual relations by creating zones of noncompetition.
Moreover, though not always assuring their security, sovereignty has
empowered small states by defining their legitimate rights and providing access to international decision-making.[4]

The principle of nonintervention is a pivotal corollary of sovereignty doctrine, as it excludes other powers from the internal sphere
of a state. The doctrine of nonintervention can be justly criticized
for ignoring the gross violations of human rights, democracy, and

peace within a state, which possibly could be stopped by external intervention. Yet, the frequent resort to humanitarian intervention would, in many cases, violate the rights of people and erode international order.[5]

Therefore, humanitarian intervention is a tool which should be used parsimoniously, not because it may violate the norm of sovereignty, but because it may have negative and unanticipated social consequences. Other authors, while recognizing the need of autonomy by political communities, have suggested that the attitudes towards humanitarian intervention should be more permissive. It should be disengaged from the statist manner of thinking and justified by the need to honor common moral standards in international life. Thus, humanitarian intervention should obey the moral imperative rather than political expediency.[6]

The representatives of states, who in fact derive their power from the principle of sovereignty, tend to stress its external, negative aspects. The only positive aspect they usually have in mind is the legal equality of states, and thus the rights of their elites, irrespective of the physical size, ideological orientation, or the racial composition of the state. In that sense the doctrine of sovereignty is genuinely universalist, which creates an interesting tension with its particularist applications in political practice.

In assessing the value and relevance of sovereignty, one has to recall, as Jean Bethke Elshtain does, that it has deep roots in the history of constitutional and political theories. Its history provides ideas for the positive uses of sovereignty as a guarantee of both collective and individual equality and autonomy. Sovereignty may be an obstacle to an interdependent international community and conducive to power politics, but it is also a precondition for self-realization in an unequally organized international system. Thus, sovereignty is always Janus-faced.

For instance, sovereignty is a source of economic rights which assure the stable material progress of society. On the other hand, it has underpinned the development of capitalism on a national scale, which, by its very nature, engenders inequality and exploitation. Due to the intensification of economic relations and advances in technology, capitalism has become increasingly global. Globalization tends to erode the exclusive, territorial boundaries and blur the distinction between the internal and external spheres of state action. It not only reduces the autonomy of states but also induces qualitative changes in the international system, especially enhancing its non-territorial elements. Although sovereignty is a "robust concept," globalization as a multifaceted process is changing it through the redefinition of the nature and tasks of the state.[7]

The globalization argument should not be taken too far, however. Yes, globalization redefines the role of the state, but it does not eliminate the nation state and the principle of sovereignty. The social costs of globalization are so huge that an effective political unit is needed to cushion their effects on the majority of people, who suffer economically from stagnated wages or unemployment. In today's world this political unit is still the state.[8] Thus, to avoid the collapse of the world economy, globalization needs the state not only to manage social tensions engendered by it, but also to give the people a chance to participate and shape processes that directly affect them.

In other words, sovereignty has positive aspects, especially those associated with its popular roots. In effect, "sovereign equality" of states makes deeper sense only if it is underpinned by "democratic sovereignty" in which all citizens have an adequate stake. States without legitimate and effective democratic institutions tend to pose greater risks to other states; therefore, sovereignty alone cannot assure peace, but needs to be accompanied by democracy.[9]

As long as the global and regional institutions of democracy remain weak, the national participation in international decision-making, undergirded by the principle of sovereign equality, continues to be the most effective route to make people's opinions heard. From the standpoint of democratic theory and practice, sovereignty can be diminished only if regional and global democratic institutions can simultaneously be strengthened and made more accountable.[10]

The channeling of democratic participation through national governments is compatible with the view that, despite the progress of economic globalization, most aspects of international life are shaped by ever-deepening interdependence rather than truly boundary-crossing processes of integration. Even the European Union is regarded as an interdependent association of nation states rather than as a fully integrated economic and political union.[11]

Thus, sovereignty still seems to provide the most viable basis and even precondition for international influence which, in turn, can be materialized through regional and global participation of states. Abram Chayes and Antonia Handler Chayes hit the point in observing that "the only way most states can realize and express their sovereignty is through participation in the various regimes that regulate and order the international system. Isolation from the pervasive and rich international context means that the state's potential for economic growth and political influence will not be realized."[12]

Although sovereignty still matters a lot, the world seems to be torn between the national anchoring and the boundary-crossing processes of politics. These processes interact in a complex manner and encourage the rise of national constituencies which harbor different interests and values. Globalization and integration benefit young, educated, urban people, whose identities are largely non-national and non-territorial, while they are perceived as a risk by elderly, less educated, rural people, who have to adjust to new economic, social, and cultural demands. Often unable to do so, they may seek solace in territorial and local-national identities. The result is the division of society into globally networked and nationally anchored segments.[13]

It can be argued that sovereignty had its heyday during the Cold War. The fear that a conventional war would escalate into a nuclear exchange created, at least in Europe, more respect for the state borders than did any other factor. The principles of territorial status quo and of nonintervention, enshrined in the Final Act of the CSCE in 1975, permitted the socialist one-party states in Eastern and Central Europe to maintain exclusive control not only of their territories but also of their people. However, few people became attached to the one-party states, because their instrumentalism did not generate national loyalty and legitimacy. The lack of this legitimacy explains, in part, the ease of political change in most socialist states in the late 1980s.

Amplified by the risk of nuclear war, the principle of sovereignty became for the Soviet Union and its allies the first line of defense against democratization and human rights. The United States, while having encouraged the democratization of its own allies in Europe and Asia after the Second World War, never challenged the Soviet "sovereign superiority" in Eastern Europe. The Soviet Union appealed to the principle of sovereignty in defending its undemocratic domestic politics, as repeatedly as China does today.

With the Cold War gone, the nature and functions of sovereignty are changing in the former Soviet sphere of influence. Initially, the newly won independence fostered the penchant for sovereignty and national thinking, but at least among the elites it did not last long. Practically everywhere in Eastern and Central Europe it is understood that national viability can only be obtained through economic and political integration with Western multilateral institutions. "Belonging to Europe" through memberships in NATO and the European Union is more important in the Czech Republic, Hungary, and Poland than the stress on isolationist national sovereignty.

The era of parochial sovereignty and narrow-minded nationalism is largely over in Europe, although it lives in Croatia and Serbia and among the right-wing movements of the continent. Aiming at ethnical homogeneity, the elites of both Croatia and Serbia stress the uniqueness and importance of national sovereignty. Not surprisingly, such attitudes have resulted in attrocities against other national groups. The difference between Serbia and Croatia is, however, that Belgrade is uncertain about closer integration with Western Europe, while Zagreb makes an effort to combine external cooperation with the stress on nationalism and sovereignty.[14]

Jean Bethke Elshtain makes a major contribution both to political theory and political practice by stressing that the extreme interpretations of sovereignty and nationalism are unhelpful and even dangerous. Instead, she argues that we need a more complex and balanced view which does justice to sovereignty and nationalism as sources of protection and identities, but avoids entrapping us in the political cage of narrow-minded interpretations.

This call is compatible with the idea that sovereignty, indeed, has a dual character; deeper participation in the global economic system constrains the domestic decision-making of states, but also helps them to acquire resources by which sovereignty can be realized and expressed.[15] Thus, states are at the same time sovereign and non-sovereign.

NOTES

1. Tamaž Mastnak, "Fascists, Liberals, and Anti-Nationalism," in Richard Kaplan and John Feffer, eds., *Europe's New Nationalism: States and Minorities in Conflict* (Oxford: Oxford University Press, 1996), p. 62.

2. Hendrik Spruyt, *The Sovereign State and Its Competitors: An Analysis of Social Change* (Princeton, N.J.: Princeton University Press, 1994).

3. This theme is further developed by Michael Ignaticff, "Nationalism and Toleration," in *Europe's New Nationalism*, pp. 213-231.

4. See Christopher Clapham, *Africa and the International System: The Politics of State Survival* (Cambridge: Cambridge University Press, 1997), pp. 16-19, 41-43.

5. Friedrich Kratochwil, "Sovereignty as Dominium: Is There a Right for Humanitarian Intervention?" in Gene M. Lyons and Michael Mastanduno, eds., *Beyond Westphalia? State Sovereignty and International Intervention* (Baltimore, Md.: The Johns Hopkins University Press, 1995), pp. 21-42.

6. Bhikhu Parekh, "Rethinking Humanitarian Intervention," *International Political Science Review* 18, no. 1 (1997), pp. 49-69.

7. Marc Williams, "Rethinking Sovereignty," in Eleonore Kofman and Gillian Youngs, eds., *Globalization: Theory and Practice* (London: Pinter, 1996), pp. 109-137.

8. Robert Boyer, "State and Market: A New Engagement for the Twenty-First Century," in Robert Boyer and Daniel Drache, eds., *States Against Markets: The Limits of Globalization* (London: Routledge, 1996), pp. 84-114.

9. Samuel Barkin, "Legitimate Sovereignty and Risky States," in Gerald Schneider and Patricia A. Weitsman, eds., *Enforcing Cooperation: Risky States and Intergovernmental Management of Conflict* (London: Macmillan, 1997), pp. 16-36.

10. For pleas for more effective regional and global democratic institutions, respectively, see Robert A. Dahl, "A Democratic Dilemma: System Effectiveness versus Democratic Participation," *Political Science Quarterly* 109, no. 1 (1994), pp. 23-34, and David Held, "Democracy from City-States to a Cosmopolitan Order," in David Held, ed., *Prospects for Democracy: North, South, East, West* (Cambridge: Polity Press, 1993), pp. 13-52.

11. Alan S. Milward et al., eds., *The Frontier of National Sovereignty: History and Theory 1945-1992* (London: Routledge, 1992).

12. Abram Chayes and Antonia Handler Chayes, *The New Sovereignty: Compliance with International Regulatory Agreements* (Cambridge, Mass.: Harvard University Press, 1995), p. 27.

13. Mary Kaldor, "Cosmopolitanism versus Nationalism: The New Divide," in *Europe's New Nationalism,* pp. 42–58.

14. Michael Ignatieff, "Nationalism and Toleration," in *Europe's New Nationalism,* pp. 219–220.

15. Naeem Inayatullah, "Beyond Sovereignty Dilemma: Quasi-states as Social Construct," in Thomas J. Biersteker and Cynthia Weber, eds., *State Sovereignty as Social Construct* (Cambridge: Cambridge University Press, 1996), pp. 51–59.

THE 1996 HESBURGH LECTURES ON ETHICS AND PUBLIC POLICY

New Wine and Old Bottles:
International Politics and Ethical Discourse

Jean Bethke Elshtain

Prologue

WHAT'S ETHICAL
ABOUT PUBLIC POLICY?

A POWERFUL STRAND IN Western thinking about politics holds that the political and the ethical realms not only can but must be kept at arm's length. Contemporary advocates of this view of politics as a sphere of power in which the only constraint is counterforce trace their pedigree to Machiavelli and, before him, to Thucydides. The *locus classicus* of this so-called "realist" or "realpolitik" posture is the Melian dialogue in Thucydides' great masterwork, *The Peloponnesian Wars,* in which the Athenian generals tell the beleaguered representatives of the city of Melos, in effect, that "Might makes Right." The powerful do what they can; the weak suffer what they must. Machiavelli, of course, is full of delicious tales along these lines. Now, of course, there is much more to Thucydides and to Machiavelli and to all the others enshrined in the canon of realism than this sort of thing. One might argue, as I and others have, that an overly simplistic reading of the great realists yields a theory with too few categories and concepts to do justice to the complexity of international politics. We know that relations between states display many features and nuances not captured in the notion of an international free-fire zone or a calculus of the configuration of forces arrayed this way or that, to someone's benefit and someone else's disadvantage. There is something akin to what Hedley Bull called an "international society," a world in which relations between political entities are governed by norms and rules and not just by force. The context for the conduct of international relations is not a world of thoroughgoing anarchy but, rather, a world laced through and through with historically constituted and reconstituted understandings, rules, and notions about what is or is not a clear-cut (as

3

opposed to a murky) occasion for reaction and response ranging from diplomacy to alliances to boycotts to war.

A number of the important thinkers usually located as realists understood this. Max Weber, for example, made the observation a long time ago that if you have a policy of pure interest severed from ethics, things get brutal and opportunistic too easily. As well, if you promulgate a policy that's too "idealistic," severed from interests, it becomes naive, even utopian rather quickly. To bring these together in a fruitful mix would seem to be the challenge, on the level of theory and practice alike. My aspirations, theoretically speaking, are modest: I would like to call them realistic. I have long argued that there can be no grand, formalizable, universal theory of international politics.[1] The will to theorize, if undertaken with relentless solemnity as a quest for an overarching schema or Archimedean point from which the theorist can survey all he or she beholds and issue predictions, is not only unachievable in principle; it yields, at best, elegant formulations that tell us precious little about the inelegant, messy, dense, historically suffused world of international politics. This holds no matter what one's theoretical orientation, whether realist or some other.

If the entire world is not a Hobbesian battlefield in which state behavior becomes predictable in light of a few general assumptions, it is certainly no paradise or school of virtue either. Thus, one cannot blanket the world of international politics with ethical normativity. For one thing, matters are not, and can never be, under such complete control as that. We couldn't enforce an international Kantianism in a tight and total sense no matter how hard we tried. As well, the use of force isn't necessarily an ethical lapse; indeed force may sometimes be used in the name of justice. That, for example, is the whole burden carried by the "just war" tradition. To be sure, violence in this tradition is always put on trial; always placed under suspicion. The resort to force is a last resort, not a first option. The reason for this is not just a prudential one, although prudence is far better than recklessness in these matters. No, the reason lies in the explicit acknowledgment of certain ethical constraints.

My aim in these lectures is to draw the ethical and the political into a complex relationship with one another—not in the sense that there are two meticulously demarcated spheres that must be delicately pushed together, rather like porcupines greeting one another, but in a far more robust way. For politics and ethics are and always have been mutually constitutive activities. Those who have severed them utterly have laid waste towns and cities and countries and even continents. Those who collapse them into one another have done less direct damage but have also had little direct political impact, living, as they do, in a realm of ethics that is sanitized from real politics. Politics, whether domestic or international, has to do with power. Not power *über alles*, God forbid, but power as *primus inter pares*—hopefully power deployed to promote a common good; to help to create more decent and generous societies. We cannot understand the extraordinary changes of 1989 without thinking about the triumph of ethical resistance to tyrannical power. We cannot come to grips with the many currents rushing pell-mell and helter-skelter in our world at century's end without thinking about just how weak ethical condemnation of horrific events often seems if sturdy action does not flow from it. How do we put the two together in a way that is, yes, realistic yet hopeful—hopeful that human beings are capable of responding to calls to brotherhood and sisterhood, even as we know all too well that they are too often seduced by hate-mongers and fear-peddlers. That is the challenge addressed in these reflections on international politics and ethical discourse as we near the millennium.

1

SOVEREIGNTY AT CENTURY'S END

W HEN WE THINK of states we think of sovereignty. The locu-
tion—the sovereign state—springs readily to our lips. That
this is so is in some ways remarkable. The sovereignty of political
bodies is a particular historic creation. But sovereignty, encoded and
ongoingly reproduced, came to seem something of an inevitability
were a state to attain its full stature and recognition in a world of
states. Sovereignty is the insignia of membership in the club. Sovereignty at century's end remains the "essential qualification for full
membership in international society, or, to express the point more
comprehensively, the qualification which makes a state eligible for
full membership."[2] Given this fact, sovereignty serves as a goad
to political action for those peoples who have not yet attained full
international recognition. How did sovereignty become so pervasive and so perduring a feature of international relations? The answer, unsurprisingly, is tremendously complex. In order to explore
the matter, it is helpful to begin by taking up the ways in which
alternatives to sovereignty are most commonly presented.

For those who yearn for a universal order, a new and better *Pax
Romana*, sovereignty embodies a sullied and destructive particularism. They seek a more cosmopolitan scheme of things, perhaps a
universal political regime that guarantees peace by stripping individual political bodies of one central feature of sovereignty—the
right to declare war should one's security or territory be threatened.
Mind you, sovereignty doesn't really go away in such visions. It is
lofted upward, escaping the confines of the state to take up residence
in the rarefied temples of a universal order. This is an unattractive
and even pernicious idea to defenders of sovereignty, for in their
eyes, sovereignty is the best way human beings have devised to create

and to defend diverse cultures and the integrity of particular peoples and their histories. They ask: Would not a universal order that presupposed for its attainment the destruction of state sovereignty become a tyranny of a sort hitherto unknown, even in the darkest moments of mid-twentieth-century totalitarianism?

If the universal alternative to particular sovereignties is an entity of sufficient power to keep all the kingdoms under its thumb, to stop all war, and to defend all those who present grievances, that would be a concentration of power awesome and terrifying to behold. And there would be no power to check that awesome power should it become overweening, suppressive, and destructive in its urge to homogenize, the better to control. Why isn't this endorsement of a new and better *Pax Romana* a recipe for legitimation of hegemony? Who sets the terms for the new universalism? How is such an escape from the perils of state sovereignty to be specified meaningfully in political institutions and life? Perhaps the defender of state sovereignty against sovereign universalism would recall the warning of Hannah Arendt from *Men in Dark Times*. Arendt wrote:

> Nobody can be a citizen of the world as he is the citizen of his country. . . . The very notion of one sovereign force ruling the whole earth, holding the monopoly of all means of violence, unchecked and uncontrolled by other sovereign powers, is not only a forbidding nightmare of tyranny, it would be the end of all political life as we know it. Political concepts are based on plurality, diversity, and mutual limitations. A citizen is by definition a citizen among citizens of a country among countries. . . . Philosophy may conceive of the earth as the homeland of mankind and of one unwritten law, eternal and valid for all. Politics deals with men, nationals of many countries and heirs to many pasts; its laws are the positively established fences which hedge in, protect, and limit the space in which freedom is not a concept, but a living, political reality. The establishment of one sovereign world state, far from being the prerequisite for world citizenship, would be the end of all citizenship.[3]

And it is the case that for Václav Havel, Lech Wałęsa, and other leaders of the democratic independence movements that spearheaded the peaceful revolutions against Soviet domination, any endorsement of such a universal order is a recipe for hegemony. Those just now tasting the fruits of political independence after a half-century of domination are unlikely to be persuaded by attacks on sovereignty as run-amok particularism, even the political triumph of a malevolent, masculinized "war-system."[4] What they know instead is that they were forced for years, under the heel of Communist 'universalism', to crush difference, "to make everything the same." Writes Havel: "The greatest enemy of communism was always individuality, variety, difference—in a word, freedom. From Berlin to Vladivostok, the streets and buildings were decorated with the same red stars. Everywhere the same celebratory parades were staged. Analogical state administrations were set up, along with the whole system of central direction for social and economic life. This vast shroud of uniformity, stifling all national, intellectual, spiritual, social, cultural, and religious variety, covered over any differences and promoted the monstrous illusion that we were all the same."[5]

Now, the critic of sovereignty could bounce back in this way. He or she could argue that sovereignty is itself a form of homogenization and hegemony. Doesn't the sovereign state operate under an urgent imperative to make everything internal to its borders 'the same'? Just follow the trail of human tears. How many indigenous peoples have been wiped out or shoved into nooks and crannies in the wider order? How many immigrants to new countries have found and continue to find themselves under assault as threats to the political order? In the United States in the World War I era, a veritable orgy of anti-immigrant hysteria swept the land, fueled (alas) by the highest reaches of government including President Woodrow Wilson. Perhaps offering a flavor of that moment shows the drive to internal homogeneity that has certainly been one pervasive feature of sovereign bodies historically.

We learn that the history of the United States is not entirely reassuring on precisely this score. A case in point is the sustained attack on so-called "hyphenated Americans" in the World War I era. In 1917, President Woodrow Wilson committed himself to universal conscription, not just for defense in case of the outbreak of hostilities but to help mold a new nation. Two years before the United States entered the war, Wilson himself had attacked hyphenated

Americans in harsh words: "There are citizens of the United States, I blush to admit, born under other flags, but welcomed under our generous naturalization laws to the full freedom and opportunity of America, who have poured the poison of disloyalty into the very arteries of our national life. . . . Such creatures of passion, disloyalty, and anarchy must be crushed out. . . . The hand of our power should close over them at once."[6] Congress responded in kind by passing legislation to check espionage and treason that vested the government with powers to censor the press, to punish interference with activities of the armed services, including recruitment, and to control the mails to prevent dissemination of allegedly treasonable material—all measures subject to a laxity of interpretation and temptation to abuse. Vigilantism against alleged slackers and traitors received public sanction. The lynching of Robert Prager, a young German-born immigrant who had tried to enlist in the American Navy but had been rejected for medical reasons, took place before a cheering crowd of nearly five hundred souls near St. Louis, Missouri. When the leaders of the lynch mob were tried, their defense counsel called their offense "patriotic murder," and a jury returned a not guilty verdict. Even those who deplored such excesses contributed to the public mood by attacking all who raised questions about the wisdom of American entry into the war.

A dream of unity lurks here. In the minds of the architects of national unity through what I have called elsewhere *armed civic virtue,* the presence of millions of immigrants was an ongoing irritant. "Americanization" became the goal, the watchword; for some, the threat: one nation indivisible. To be sure, genuine regard for the welfare of immigrant groups lay at the base of much sentiment, including that expressed by the National American Woman Suffrage Association, which believed that separatism and heterogeneity were synonymous with inequality and marginality. But progressive and liberal opinion proved particularly susceptible to the cry for unity because of its stress on popular sovereignty and its embrace of the notion that there must be some strong civic glue to bind the nation as one. As notable a figure as the great philosopher and progressive, John Dewey, could wax eloquent about the war's "social possibilities."

In light of these and other historic examples, many of them far
worse, the critic of sovereignty would have a pretty strong case, it
seems, in urging that sovereignty's excesses have been so common
they appear to go with the territory, quite literally. But to reach this
conclusion would be to ignore the extraordinary richness of constitutionalism and the intricate, elaborate, and powerful ways that sovereignty domestically has been check-mated in the West and is being
circumscribed in many of the newly emergent democracies through
the codification of human rights, separation of powers, representa-
tive government, due process, protection of minorities, and other
features of constitutionalism with which we are familiar. So we can
guard against the internal excesses, the defender would say. *State* and
sovereignty do not form an unproblematic unity.

This wouldn't be nearly enough of a concession to a strong critic
of sovereignty, one, let's say, who celebrates a principle of difference
rather than universalism as the best way to organize political life.
For example, there are contemporary multiculturalists who want
more fragmentation; more representations of diversity; a veritable
festival of officially recognized differences. They aver that in a political world dominated by mutual claims to recognition, sovereignty would simply become supererogatory; other ways of forg-
ing political bodies would have been achieved through what might
be called plural constitutionalisms and, in some cases, separatism.
The defender of sovereignty at this juncture would surely charge the
multiculturalist with his or her own form of absolutism—absolutizing the principle of difference—and, as well, presupposing for the
fleshing out of his or her ideal the very thing sovereignty provides—
a regime of civic order and domestic peace, however rambunctious
the democratic contestations. For multicultural engagements can
only be peaceful and relatively benign when their excesses are, in
principle, checkable and when the engagements themselves are
structured and mediated by countervailing political forces. Otherwise one winds up not with a "relatively peaceful coat of many col-
ors," in Isaiah Berlin's phrase, but with Balkanization, an old term
that has, alas, become apt once again. I will have more to say on this
problem in chapter 2 below, but it is important to note here that if

a temptation of sovereignty has been a search for absolute mastery over spatial territory, a danger in deconstructing sovereignty altogether in favor of what is always presented as a more benign alternative is that civic order itself comes under siege. You don't have to be Machiavelli to fret about the political naivete embedded in some multicultural visions. ·

As we can readily see, sovereignty ongoingly generates a number of difficult problems: questions of universalism and particularism; definitions of international relations in terms of the presence of sovereign states as primary actors while the "system itself" is defined by the absence of sovereignty. The historic discourse of sovereignty is a formulation of mastery over internal or domestic space and vulnerability in the external zone of competing sovereignties. Alternatives to sovereignty as traditionally and currently presented are either a cure through a thorough-going universalism or else shock treatment by getting more of what sovereignty fears—more competing political or identity groups with strong claims to recognition. Such alternatives trail in their wake a whole series of other, seemingly insuperable problems. So are we just stuck with sovereignty? Why do our choices so often seem so extreme—either two hundred sovereignties vying with one another in a competitive field, or the imperial or transnational supercession of sovereignty, or quickening the pace of political particularism? Perhaps a brief genealogical reconstruction of sovereignty's sway will help us to understand its ascendancy and its continuing hold on our politics and our political imaginations.

Sovereignty is a heroic narrative, a story of the bringing of order and civic peace and unity, on the one hand, and of the inevitability of war and state violence, on the other. This narrative gained ascendancy as a particular historic configuration, a response to concrete pressures and problems. How come? For one thing, the way was paved by historic transformations in Western theology of the *imago Dei* or image of God. My argument will be that political meanings in the West got layered over potent images of the sacred. Indeed, the OED reflects this by showing that *power* as a characteristic of political or national strength is a "late use" preceded by "a celestial or spiritual being having control or influence; a divinity." Claims to earthly power or *potestas* as dominion and rule are themselves parasitic upon constructions of a sovereign deity for much of their force.

I want to be careful here. There is no single *imago Dei* that dominated Western Christian theology. Prior to the Reformation, God was construed as relational (three persons in one) and as the site of an amplitude of reason; a fullness of Being; a plenitude and lushness of power. God brought forth all the things that swim, and creep and crawl, and fly. Man (male and female) become somewhat akin to God in several senses, theologically speaking. We are created in God's image. But after the Fall, we also take upon ourselves certain godlike powers. In some sense we begin to act like God: man (plural as male and female) as co-creators. This gets us into heavy theological waters pretty fast but I hope you will follow me for a moment or two as I try to shed light on just how the extraordinary powers we attribute to sovereigns and sovereignties came into being.

Although the human being becomes godlike he or she remains under God's sovereign dominion. In post-Occam theology (this means after the fourteenth century), God is less and less represented as the fullness of reason and goodness in His relational complexity and more and more embodied as the site of sovereign *will*. God's volitionality trumps other features of the *imago Dei*. A monistic conception partially squeezes our more relational understandings. God's power in this vision is not only absolute but even somewhat arbitrary. God's right is coterminous with His sovereign power: it is a right of dominion, rule, possession, "all-pervasive and efficient . . . omnipotent and undefeatable."[7] This vision came to dominate sovereignty talk and helped to lay the basis for the juristic conception of the state, when man decided he, too, could be sovereign in this way. Writes the controversial German theorist Carl Schmitt, "All significant concepts were transferred from theology to the theory of the state, whereby, for example, the omnipotent God became the omnipotent lawgiver . . . the recognition of which is necessary for a sociological consideration of these concepts."[8]

In my book, *Women and War*, I wrote about "the Protestant Nation-State," for it is only with the break-up of medieval Christendom, the shift to post-Occam theologies, and the reemergence of

Roman private law as a law for centralizing monarchies, that the architecture of the early modern nation-state really comes into focus. The first completely developed theory of sovereignty is Jean Bodin's *Six Books of the Commonwealth*. Sovereignty is the *summum imperium* (rumblings from the Roman Empire can be heard in the background at this point), that which can neither be delegated nor divided. "Sovereignty is that absolute and perpetual power vested in a commonwealth which in Latin is termed *majestas* . . . it is the distinguishing mark of the sovereign that he cannot in any way be subject to the commands of another, for it is he who makes law for the subject, abrogates law already made, and amends obsolete law. . . . "[9] Thomas Hobbes, in his masterwork, *The Leviathan*, depicts the sovereign's awesome sway in nonpareil terms, this from chapters 17 and 18 respectively: "The only way to erect such a Common Power . . . is to conferre all their power and strength upon one Man, or upon one Assembly of men, that may reduce all their Wills . . . unto one Will. . . . This is more than Consent or Concord; it is a reall Unitie of them all, in one and the same Person. . . . This is the Generation of that Great Leviathan, or rather (to speak more reverently) of that Mortall God, to which wee owe under the Immortall God, our peace and defense. . . . And that he carryeth this Person, is called Soveraigne, and said to have Soveraigne Power; and every one besides, his Subject. . . . "[10]

Hobbes, and Bodin before him, helped to give centralizing monarchies a potent theoretical justification and rationale.[11] The difference between the powers they enumerated for the earthly sovereign, and God's, is that the earthly Sovereign, although untrammeled (more or less) in his power in a territorial space is, in the final analysis, subject to God's grace or judgment. But this divine check becomes ever more anemic. For having taken unto himself all the features of the deity, save individual immortality—although the King-dom is perpetual, hence immortality is in some sense assured—there is precious little constraint in these classic formulae on the sovereignty of the *dominus* over a bounded earthly territory, an extended "domestic" space.[12] The Thomistic denial of absolute sovereign power to any of the component communities of Christendom, including papacy and empire, gives way to the construction of a perpetual, supreme power, a King's body that could not be dismembered. The Sovereign becomes the final judge. All in all, these are remarkable developments, and explanations for the emergence of sovereign triumphalism tend to fall into two broad categories, each at once explanation and justification, and each ignoring the theological backdrop.

The first explanation holds that in situations of sometimes terrible disorder, with chaos threatening, guaranteed order and civic peace, at whatever price, become overriding imperatives. The fragmentation and chaos (in a negative characterization) of medieval Europe, divided as it was into too many kingdoms under the overarching (if underawing) Holy Roman Empire, with the pope meddling as well, are most often cited as an explanation of the need for sovereign states. For the medieval system was "a patchwork of overlapping and incomplete rights of government . . . inextricably superimposed and tangled" with different "juridical instances . . . geographically interwoven and stratified, . . . plural allegiances, asymmetrical suzerainties and anomalous enclaves" abounding.[13] Is this any way to run a continent? The sovereigntists answered with a resounding "no" and the nation state was off and running. Thus the defenders of the move toward state sovereignty reason.

The second explanation, and one having greater plausibility, remarks that the rediscovery "from Roman law of the concept of absolute private property and the simultaneous emergence of mutually exclusive territorial state formations" go together. Rome transmitted the concept of the sovereign in terms of the emperor's *imperium* to the Middle Ages. But this redolent little seed didn't germinate meaningfully until legists, mostly French, crystallized the idea of state sovereignty with metahistorical justification drawn from Roman law and imperial practice.[14] One brief example, a 1443 statement updating Roman law from Bologna University, famous for its law school, claims, in part: "There is one judge from whom the final decision of cases comes, lest with many judges contending, and no one supreme, litigations would never be finished. Also, no family, no community, no kingdom can remain in its full *status,* unless it has one supreme ruler; because from divisions of heads there easily arises division and schism among the members."[15] The king becomes emperor in his kingdom and the formulation *rex imperator et regno suo* is laid on, becoming especially potent when combined with the *cujus regio* rule of Augsburg.

The standard narrative, or classical theory, then, holds that sovereignty is indivisible and inalienable. It defines the supreme, the *above* all else. This is far more than a legal theory or task. It involves notions of civic order, identity, and images of well-being or danger. Sovereignty shifts from king to state and the state "can no more alienate its sovereignty than a man can alienate his will and remain a man."[16] Hendrik Spruyt's recent work, *The Sovereign State and Its Competitors,* underscores these points. He remarks that the choice of French kings to favor Roman law as the basis of political authority involved a "staggering shift of beliefs." For Roman law was radically different from the legal systems of German and Frankish tribes. It departed from the particularism induced by feudalism. As well, the idea of exclusive authority over territorial space corresponded with the definition of property rights in Roman law. The medieval idea of possession, by contrast, was embedded in a network of overlapping rights and claims. The content of Christian doctrine was biased against private property. Roman law, by contrast, granted to the owner exclusive use and rights.[17] With the coming of sovereign prerogatives, all intermediate bodies and their corporate privileges came under pressure to succumb or to conform—whether cities, guilds, feudal principalities, or the Church itself.

Popular sovereignty, if anything, deepened these ideas. For example, as articulated by the architects of the terror during the French Revolution, popular sovereignty constituted internal enemies on a par with external foes. The Jacobin Committee of Public Safety, identifying its will with the general will, declared: "Whereas the French people has manifested its will, everyone who is opposed to it is outside its sovereignty; everyone outside the sovereignty is an enemy. . . . Between the people and its enemies, there is nothing in common but the sword."[18] Notice that sovereignty in this construction redefines the boundaries. The rule of force ordinarily reserved to foreigners now pertains among citizens. There is no appeal to any higher court than the sovereign, and if this sovereign is identified with "the people," and certain persons or groups are declared

no longer part of the people, then they, too, become foreigners—
even worse, enemies. One distinguishing mark of the sovereign is
here articulated in its potentially most repressive form: the legal freedom of every sovereign country in the regulation of its own domestic affairs. "There is no appeal to any higher court," writes Arnold Brecht, "no arbiter, avenger or ultimate guardian of peace and
justice."[19]

Where does this leave us? Even those who lament the excesses of
sovereignty, whether in its monarchical, statist, or popular forms,
cannot, it seems, do without it. All critiques take it on as a point of
reference if not a starting point. Indeed, it is the least interesting
treatments of the theme that simply condemn sovereignty and move
on to construct an imagined world that would come into being were
it dissolved altogether. Knowing, as we do, that sovereignty is supreme and that the state as an independent, territorial monopoly of
political power triumphed historically, does not commit us to the
tacit teleology embodied in F. H. Hinsley's declaration that sovereignty is the culmination of a movement of something akin to historic inevitability. The concept was "sooner or later unavoidable
because men have thought of power in terms of sovereignty," he
writes, and because human beings experience "a primary need to
insure effective exercise of power. . . . " It follows that we have little
choice but to stick with sovereignty for one very good reason: "The
internal mechanism of the modern body politic would grind to a
halt if the assumption that there was a final and absolute authority
within it were to be abandoned. In international practice the existence of a sovereign authority within the separate community is uni-
versally recognized as the essential qualification of its membership
in the international community. . . . "[20] Hinsley's beginning point
and end point come full circle. A pre-given set of needs (for the final
say, for effective exercise of power) dictates an end (state sovereignty). Or, as Luther might quip, "Frogs need storks." Sovereignty
is both a first principle and a necessity.

Although classical liberal theorists are less preoccupied with sovereignty than with the terms under which a civic order can, in some
sense, be said to be both robust and limited by law and the action
of citizens, they, too, remain preoccupied with who shall have the

final say in matters of dispute. In and through a complicated set of
historic transformations that cannot be unpacked here in any detail,
constitutionalism emerged in a way that called democratic republics
into being yet built in limits to the sway of sovereign excess *internally*—constraints all too often transgressed, as my example from
World War I in the United States above reminds us. But at water's
edge, the full panoply of pre-constitutional sovereignty kicks in.
The United States Supreme Court weighed in early, tipping the
scales toward a strong definition of *external* sovereignty. An early
court decision, *Chisholm v. Georgia* (1793), includes Justice Wilson's
famous words: "To the Constitution of the United States the term
sovereign is totally unknown. There is but one place where it could
have been used with propriety. But, even in that place, it would not,
perhaps, have comported with the delicacy of those who ordained
and established that constitution. They might have announced
themselves 'sovereign' people of the United States: But serenely con-
scious of the fact, they avoided the ostentatious declaration."[21] But
just nineteen years later, in *The School Exchange v. M'Faddon* (1812),
Chief Justice Marshall embraces the ostentatious version of sovereignty as a territorial *imprimatur:* "The jurisdiction of the nation within its own territory is necessarily exclusive and absolute.
It is susceptible of no limitation not imposed by itself. Any restric-
tion upon it, deriving validity from an external source, would
imply a diminution of its sovereignty to the extent of the restric-
tion. . . . "[22] A 1936 decision, *U.S. v. Curtiss-Wright Export Corp,* re-
affirms Marshall: "Rules come and go; governments end and forms
of government change; but sovereignty survives. A political society
cannot endure without a supreme will somewhere. Sovereignty is
never held in suspense."[23] Sovereignty takes on a kind of metaphysi-
cal status here—"it" exists whether an actual political body does or
not. A government may go. But sovereignty perdures. Here sovereignty as a first principle trumps any argument from necessity or,
perhaps better, the two are fused—political society cannot be en-
sured without a supreme will.

One final brief restatement of the classical theory, then: (a) internally, sovereignty is the power to order a domestic arena without
external interference, (b) externally, sovereign power exists in a sys-

tem of at least theoretical independence and equality whose relations are controlled by principles of force as the court of last resort.
Central to this classical account are ideas drawn from Roman law. I
have already mentioned one—the Roman law of private property.
But there is another point to be made, that of "legal subjectivity,"
lodged in two carriers: the *paterfamilias*, and the force of command
or will in law, *jus*, derived from the *populus Romanus* construed as
a unified subject. Just as the *paterfamilias* were the "sole, self-deter-
mined, and in their sphere sovereign representative(s) of right," so
the "multiplicity of equal wills" composed of all multiple "fathers"
culminated in a center of "common legal subjectivity," the will or
voice of the abstract, collective legal personality.[24]

We are a long way indeed from the Roman *dominus* in late modern industrial Western societies, but traces of this construction
appear in all early modern theories of sovereignty and are borne
forward to the present. Consider, if you will, the fact that one overarching preoccupation of sovereigntists is the setting of boundaries,
especially between the "domestic" and the "foreign." The domestic
arena is a particularly fascinating field to explore. For domesticity is
the realm we usually associate with woman. The word comes from
the Latin, *domesticus, domus*, and it is "of or pertaining to the
household or family, as domestic duties." This suggests that the do-
mestication of the household is a central if under-theorized and
submerged feature of the classical theory of sovereignty. Roman private law, remember, is a law of absolute possession, always amelio-
rated in practice and always involving requirements for provision as
well as sanctifications for power.

But perhaps this Roman law backdrop and the domestic origins
of our notion of state sovereignty—if my hunch bears any critical
weight—help us to understand the preoccupation of sovereigntists
historically with a unified will. There must be one voice, one final
will brought to bear against cacophony and chaos. As the singularity
of God's will prevails in the post-Occam *imago Dei*, so must the
Sovereign's will be singular and his power irresistible. For Bodin,
the family lacks perpetual and absolute sovereignty, being a "right
ordering of a group of persons owing obedience to the head of a
household," but a commonwealth is the right ordering of a number

of families by a sovereign power. The two are analogized and within the family, as within the commonwealth, power is singular, deriving from the head. The power, authority, and command a husband has over his wife is, according to Bodin, "allowed by both divine and positive law to be honourable and right," and the father alone has a "natural right to command," standing as he does in the image of God. Hobbes gives dominion to both husband and wife but the family lacks sovereignty and is not, for him, a major concern; however, the masculinized face of the Sovereign is retained. This "personalization of sovereign power arose out of a continuation of the arguments from unity and peace. . . . It achieves this purpose of providing a point of resolution for the conflicts arising within a society."[25]

As I suggested above, even liberal theorists who reject strong dominion theories in the pre-constitutional tradition remain concerned with who shall have final say in matters of dispute. Although the master of the family lacks the sterner attributes of the Roman *pater*, and although his role and identity are much softened and chastened given Christian notions of stewardship, partnership, mutual marital fidelity, and the like, still, order is needed and in a case of marital dissension, rule "naturally falls to Man's share as the abler and stronger"—or so insisted Jeremy Bentham, who goes on to offer a rather homey example on settling competition between husband and wife over whether the meat shall be boiled or roasted. Finally, someone has got to decide or we should never eat dinner! This leads to his insistence that the "Man's share" prevails.[26]

This but scratches the surface on a topic on which gallons of ink have been spilled, to which thousands of trees have sacrificed their lives, but more importantly, one that is arguably at the heart of many of our troubled globe's most horrific atrocities as well as its most glorious achievements. Sovereignty is no simple matter. If that were the case, one could celebrate or condemn and have done with it. This the careful critic cannot do. But there is much to be done. I will conclude this first lecture by offering up intimations of ways to continue to plumb the depths of our indebtedness to sovereignty and to explore directions for rethinking power and the creation and sustenance of political bodies in late modernity.

First, because power lies at the heart of the matter, any critical
unpacking of sovereignty must reveal how power is understood
within sovereign discourse—both understood and constituted, it
must be said. All political theorists are familiar with Hannah Arendt's
worthy effort to rescue politics from war by severing power from
violence. According to Arendt, by conflating the crude instrumentalism of violence with power itself, defined by Arendt as the human
ability to act in concert and to begin anew, we guarantee further
loss of space within which authentic politics is possible. In this way
violence nullifies power and stymies political being. This is provocative—Arendt is always provocative—but by no means unproblematic. For when it comes to relations between states, Arendt simply
throws up her hands and opts for the Hobbesian war of all against
all, or so it seems. She notes offhandedly that we have wars because
"there is no final arbiter in international affairs." To be sure, she
decries the "sovereignty of the state" as the source of this Hobbesian nightmare. But that is as far as it goes, despite the fact that
she declares the "identification of freedom with sovereignty" to be
"perhaps the most pernicious and dangerous consequence of the
political equation of freedom and free will," adding that the "famous sovereignty of political bodies has always been an illusion,
which, moreover, can be maintained only by instruments of violence, that is, with essentially nonpolitical means." It follows that
if men "wish to be free, it is precisely sovereignty they must renounce."[27]

This is a terribly underdeveloped feature of Arendt's political
thought that awaits further elaboration. Perhaps, in the context of
the United States, exploring the distinction Sanford Levinson marks
between the constitution identified with the "sovereign will of the
people" (he cites the case *Prigg v. Pennsylvania,* which upheld the
1793 fugitive slave act) and, by contrast, the constitution as a guarantor of justice would clarify matters and help us to appreciate the
role of constitutionalism in either buttressing or ameliorating the
classical theory and practice of sovereignty. But it would just skate
on the surface of Arendt's arguments concerning politics, power,
and action. What might flesh this out with some degree of robustness would be locating a number of really good examples that dem-

onstrate the ways in which presuppositions of sovereignty quashed political action and destroyed authentic power in the Arendtian sense and, by contrast, a number of examples showing the ways in which less overweening notions of political incorporation and independence opened up space for political action. Under what circumstances does constitutionalism hold sovereigntist imperatives in check and when does this not happen? Given the realist insight that the strong are more likely to dominate the weak where rules, regulations, norms, constraints, and punishments do not exist, how are errant bullies reigned in? What checks states that themselves become bullies? Are we just inevitably drawn back into the agonistic arena of multiple, competing sovereignties in which an association of "good states" must ally to check the behavior of a "bad state"? Or does constitutionalism analogous to the domestic regimes of constitutional republics have a chance of replacing the world of self-help? There are dozens of studies that struggle with such questions. But the questions remain. The intractability of these matters surely has something to do with how sovereignty has been defined and enacted—set up as both first principle and tough necessity. Maybe if some of the luster were taken off the surface sheen of sovereignty, and if one could begin to view sovereignty as a practical necessity, not a sacral principle, more experimentation with alternatives that preserve a commitment to political independence and the yearning of peoples for security and stability but avoid strong sovereignty might be possible.

A second area worth exploring is the interrelationship between sovereignty on the level of states and late modern presuppositions of a sovereign self. We say states are sovereign when they decide for themselves, without interference. This has become a rough and ready operating definition of self-sovereignty. In the late modern West, we place a huge premium on autonomy understood as sovereignty. Indeed, we are urged everyday to "choose" for ourselves; not to permit others to deflect us from our chosen course; not to get so entangled in personal and familial life that we are not "free" to make the next big move, even to see ourselves as the possessors of ourselves, as owners of our own lives. Of late, even the human body itself is seen as a potential foe that we must reshape, control, dominate, manipulate. Celebrations of the brave new world of genetic engineering speak of human beings as like unto the gods, creatures who no longer need remain at the mercy of genetic accident or blind evolution. No, we can control the forces that previously controlled us. What I am suggesting is that sovereignty has once again migrated. Even as sovereignty moved from theology and the attributes of the deity to politics and the powers of the monarch or the state, what we are now witnessing is a culmination of all that harnessed definitional energy and conceptual reification in the service of a redefined self—one that is sovereign in all things. Ironically, as all sorts of voices call for us to recognize our interdependence with other nations, peoples, and states, our interdependence with those concrete human beings we call friends and family and neighbors is undermined, even negated, by calls for a fully sovereign self. To say that this matter bears further exploration is to understate.

Third and finally, can we imagine a secure politics in the absence of the strong theory and practice of sovereignty? Certainly such a politics now exists in theory. Much of the political writing by Central Europeans over the past several decades embraces precisely this possibility. I have in mind those who, before 1989, theorized civil society as an alternative to, or even in opposition to, an authoritarian sovereign state apparatus. The alternative they posed to state-dominant sovereign discourse was often quite suggestive and subtle. For example, Adam Michnik seeks to hold tradition and change, claims of community and individual freedom, and effective power and robust ethics, in fruitful tension with one another. He insists that if the state, in the name of sovereignty, intervenes decisively on one side or another in permanently contestable matters (say, community v. individual), "pluralism is destroyed."[28] Václav Havel downplays sovereignty in favor of civil society as both a domestic and international imperative, noting that perhaps states that, historically, have been more acted upon than free agents are in an ideal position to articulate an alternative to sovereigntist triumphalism.[29] A third important theorist whose work bears serious attention is Karol Wojtyła (Pope John Paul II), who has elaborated an alternative to statist versions of sovereignty, addressing the theme along these lines: "The state is firmly sovereign when it governs society and also serves the common good of society and allows the nation to realize its own subjectivity, its own identity."[30] Here the notion of sovereignty is located in neither the state per se, nor in the unmediated construction of the sovereign will of the people, but in the various associations of civil society in dialogue with one another as "subjects." This authoritative dialogue, in turn, sustains the state as an entity whose legitimate purpose is to see that rules for civility are followed and the various loci of human social existence, necessary to human dignity and freedom, are protected and served. The co-existence of overlapping, porous entities is assumed. Rights inhere in communities and groups as well as individuals; thus, more power devolves to mediating institutions or flows from them than in statist theories.

This chastened version of sovereignty is protective of plurality internally and universal aspirations externally. The possibility of agreement and alliances and agonistic encounters is always open. The state is not a hard-shelled, impermeable entity; rather, it exists in an international society in which sovereignty is necessarily limited. States are nested in wider societies, in strategic cultures, if you will. Attunement to *this* stubborn reality lends itself to an analysis at odds with all austere, de-historicized theories and accounts. For the nation-state is a phenomenon that cannot be imagined or legislated out of existence. Needing others to define ourselves, we will remain inside a state-centered discourse, for better and for worse, so long as states remain the best way we have thus far devised for protecting and sustaining a way of life in common. But taming and limiting the demands of sovereignty is a more exigent requirement than ever. I have in mind a politics that would also profoundly shift the focus of political loyalty and identity such that we would no longer be seen as civic beings mobilizable to certain ends and purposes but as citizens who are responsible to and for one another and for what they hold in common and for articulating and embodying their differences in ways that do not create enemies, in part because the presupposition of an enemy is not the place from which one starts.

Identification with a nation-state is a complex thing, tapping particularism and universalism. Indeed, one might argue that modern nation-state civic life is composed of normatively vital aspects of both ethnicity and universal values, organic integration and voluntarism. Human beings require concrete reference groups in order to attain and secure individual identity. But too complete immersion in such groups limits the boundaries of identity and identification to fixed familial, tribal, or territorial lines. What this yields is not only a complex political orientation but a subtle ethical stance, or what I have called an ethic of responsibility in contrast to the will-to-sacrifice I associate with the war and mobilization features of sovereigntist ideologies. For sovereignty historically has also called forth, even mandated, sacrifice of the most extreme sort. Softening that regime doesn't eliminate the possibility of civic duty and sacrifice but relocates it as flowing from something more akin to what Simone Weil called "love and concern" for one's country rather than from reflected glory in her triumphs and boastful puffed-up pride in her power to dominate and to control. The pre-emptory sovereign self here gives way to a vision of men and women as free citizens, standing before one another in relations of trust and arenas of struggle, sometimes at odds, sometimes shoulder to shoulder, accepting the burdens of free responsibility and undertaking tasks that are always carried out in that twilight that attends human affairs. It is a vision of a world in which sovereignty is wisely reserved to God alone, and imperfect and incomplete human beings resist the temptation to sacralize their earthly arrangements, as the classical notion of sovereignty demands they must.

2

REFLECTIONS ON
THE NEW NATIONALISM

NATIONALISM IS THE great political passion of our time. That this is so is surprising and disturbing to many. Over the years, political scientists and pundit-prognosticators predicted confidently that nationalism would cease to be a powerful force as the world moved toward triumphant rationalism. I recall listening to a talk delivered by one of the sprouts off the Huxley branch—Sir Julian, I believe—back in the 1960s. He told the students there assembled that by the year 2000, if not before, religion and nationalism would have gone the way of extinct creatures like the Tyrannosaurus Rex: safely relegated to a past from which they may titillate and even terrify us but can do us no real harm. He assumed, uncritically, that both religion and nationalism were wholly malevolent forces. What was not malevolent, what trailed only benefit in its dual wake, was the combined behemoth: science and rationalism. Well, that prediction came a cropper. We have glimpsed the dark underside to much that goes under the name of science and we have noticed that rationalism of Huxley's sort seems too thin to sustain human meaning and purpose. Be advised: this is not a brief against either science or rationalism. But it is a recognition that science breeds forms of control and feeds arrogant anthropocentrism unless it is checked by, or mingled with, other forces. Rationalism, if severed from human bodies and lived lives and complex forces, can never really come close to the whole truth of the human condition. So we are left with a world in which nationalism is not only in full flower but in which its ugliest features are daily manifest. Religious commitment, too, has shown, as it always does, its many faces—its ability to stir human beings to acts of courage and decency as well as its capacity to roil the forces of prejudice and xenophobia. Religion is not the subject of this discussion although the possibility of forgiveness, a central motif in Christian theology, will be explored in the epilogue in some detail.

But it is nationalism we are tracking. With what has been called the "new nationalism" in mind, I will explore the interwoven themes of self-identity, self-determination, and national urgency as manifest at present in the penultimate realm in which each takes shape: the world of states, would-be-states, political rule, and civic life. As we near century's end, there are some things we ought, perhaps, have learned. One is that the imperial suppression of particular national identities is costly indeed—costly, in the first instance, because of the injustices and sorrows such suppression trails in its wake; costly, in the second place, because these identities, once permitted expression, may take shape in ferocious and disturbing forms. As Sir Isaiah Berlin has noted: "People tire of being spat upon, ordered about by a superior nation, a superior class, or a superior anyone. Sooner or later, they ask the nationalist questions: 'Why do we have to obey them?' 'What about us?' "[31] In her important book on nationalism, Liah Greenfeld argues that: "National identity is, fundamentally, a matter of dignity. It gives people reasons to be proud." Peoples historically—including many of our own foremothers and forefathers—fought "over respect due to them, rather than anything else."[32] Václav Havel speaks of the "desire to renew and emphasize one's identity" as a force that lies behind "the emergence of many new countries. Nations that never had states of their own feel an understandable need to experience independence."[33] Each of these thinkers acknowledges that the nation-state model emerged historically with the Treaty of Westphalia in 1648, but this form has now been embraced or imposed worldwide. Thus, at present, aggrieved peoples want not an end to the nation-state, or to sovereignty or national autonomy, but an end to Western colonial, or Soviet, or other "external" dominance of their particular histories, languages, cultures, and wounded sense of identity.

Western religious thought has long recognized the validity and importance of self-determination, tying this concept to the need to work to achieve a common good and to a vision of human dignity tied "unquestionably," according to Pope John XXIII in *Pacem in Terris*, to the "right to take an active part in government."[34] In that great document, John XXIII reminds us that no human being is "by nature superior to his fellows, since all men are equally noble in natural dignity. And consequently there are no differences at all between political communities from the point of view of natural dignity."[35] Yet is this not what nationalism always violates by insisting that some states or peoples are in fact not only different from others, given their history and culture, but superior too? Is not the equal dignity of all peoples necessarily violated by nationalism?

George Orwell, for one, thought so. Orwell, in "Notes on Nationalism," traces the drastic simplifications and overwrought evocation of competitive prestige in which the nationalist, one who uses all "his mental energy in either boosting or in denigrating," indulges. Orwell calls such nationalist thought obsessive and indifferent to reality—persisting on a plane far removed from the concrete truths of everyday social life, which is characteristic of any ideological system. The nationalist (by contrast to the civic patriot, of whom I will say more below) classifies people like insects and assumes that "whole blocks of millions or tens of millions of people can be confidently labelled 'good' or 'bad'."[36] The nationalist insists, as well, that no other duty must be allowed to override or even challenge that to the nation-state. He evokes power as force—we need more of it, we can never have enough of it, somebody else is creeping up on us and may soon have more than we do—and he sinks his own individuality into an overarching identification with the collective. By contrast, Orwell endorsed a robust version of patriotic or civic identity, a form of identification always wary and cautious of nationalistic excess because the temptation of national identity is to push in a triumphalist direction. How do we sort this out?

Let's keep *Pacem in Terris* in mind and to it add the United States Catholic Bishops' teaching document, "A Harvest of Peace is Sown in Justice." The bishops, too, endorse self-determination and claim that it "should neither be dismissed as always harmful or unworkable nor embraced as an absolute right or a panacea in the face of injustice. . . . While full political independence may be morally right and politically appropriate in some cases, it is essential that any new state meet the fundamental purpose of sovereignty: the commitment and capacity to create a just and stable political order and to contribute to the international common good."[37] In line with their 1985 pastoral on peace and nuclear strategy, I take the bishops to be lifting up a *via media,* a moderate but firm course between the Scylla of sovereign absolutism, or an absolutizing of particular national identities, and the Charybdis of an arrogant universalism, or imperialism running roughshod over self-determination and diversity. This middle way seems so eminently reasonable, one wonders why things haven't worked out this way.

The trouble is simply endemic to identification with a collective, here the nation. In order to sustain civic life with any degree of robustness, a perceived sense of shared identity is necessary. John Keane, a British theorist of civil society, writes of just how central collective identity was to the birth of democracy. Without a "shared sense of nationhood, that is, a collective identity of people who share a language or a dialect of a common language, inhabit or are closely familiar with a defined territory, experience its ecosystem with some affection, and share a variety of customs, including a measure of memories of the historical past, which is consequently experienced in the present tense as pride in the nation's achievements and, where necessary, an obligation to feel ashamed of the nation's failings," the emergence of democracy would have been impossible.[38] Much that is good and worthy requires such shared identity.

Identification with a nation goes deep and begins early. In his work on *The Political Life of Children,* Robert Coles found attachment to a homeland, or an imagined homeland, in the symbolism and imagery deployed by children. "Nationalism works its way into just about every corner of the mind's life," Coles writes. Children have ready access to a nation's "name, its flag, its music, its currency, its slogans, its history, its political life," and this personalized yet political identity shapes their outlook and actions. Entrenched notions of a homeland are double-edged, at once inward looking, toward the place where one "gets one's bearings," and outward projecting, distinguishing and perhaps protecting "us" from "them," from foreigners who, all too easily, may become enemies. Both aspects of homeland and nationalist imagery turn up "in the developing conscience of young people" everywhere.[39] In order to get the good, one must, apparently, risk the bad, an overarching identification with one's own group that spills over into demonization of others. For we all know the troubles that national identity trails in its wake and why there is so much cause for concern.

What we have seen unfold in the Balkans is the latest concrete embodiment of a very old phenomenon, one from which our own society is by no means exempt. Whether in harsh efforts to homogenize (as in my World War I example above) or in current articulations of multiculturalism as an absolutism of particular identities, the United States has had its share of nationalistic excess, sometimes in the interest of the nation-state; sometimes in the service of a nation in opposition to the state. But any position that holds that identities must not be mixed; that, quite literally, whites and blacks, or men and women, or homosexuals and heterosexuals, inhabit incommensurable epistemological universes, is one to which the civic pluralist must take exception even as he or she also opposes those who aim to quash all articulations of difference in the interest of an overarching collective.

The civic pluralist, by contrast to nationalists whether of a statist or multiculturalist variety, embraces universalist aspirations and possibilities, affirming the idea that we can and must reach out in gestures of solidarity, friendship, and citizenship to those different from ourselves. As G. M. Tamas puts it, the "ethnocultural" version of identity and nationalism is that "others ought to be elsewhere; there is no universalistic, overriding, trans-contextual principle 'legitimising' mixture, assimilation or diversity within the same politico-symbolic 'space.' "[40] Those who break bodies politic into "warring ethnocultural enclaves" disdain nineteenth-century liberal and civic republican ideas of citizenship and dismiss the *via media* articulated within Catholic social thought. For the *via media* accepts the possibility of, and in some instances the necessity for, a form of national identity not reducible to ethnicity or culture as that which is simply given. The "new" ethnocultural nationalism, "particularly in the extreme shape it has taken in Eastern Europe, cannot and does not want to answer political questions. It is mostly a repetitive

reaffirmation of identity."[41] The only precept offered by the ethnoculturalist is: "Be what you are," as an essentialist prescription.
This, then, is by contrast to an alternative *civic* ideal, one chastened
by recognition that "others are before and among me," that I am
not hunkered down, alone, with others exactly like myself.

Warren Zimmerman, in an essay in *Foreign Affairs,* offers a
glimpse into the mind of an ethnocultural nationalist of the sort
Tamas describes. In his last talk with Serbian leader Karadzic, Zimmerman forced the question: "What sort of Bosnian Serb republic
do you have in mind? Will it be a part of Serbia?" Karadzic claims
that is for the Bosnian Serb people to decide; the first goal is independence "so we can live separately from others." Sarajevo would,
of course, be their capital. Zimmerman is perplexed, querying: "But
how can a city which is nearly 50 percent Muslim and only 30 percent
Serb be the capital for the Serbs alone?"

He continues: "Karadzic had a ready answer. 'The city will be
divided into Muslim, Serbian, and Croatian sections, so that no ethnic groups will have to live or work together.' " When pressed by
Zimmerman as to how this will be possible, Karadzic replies "matter
of factly." His answer? " 'By walls,' he said. . . . 'Of course people
will be able to pass from one part of the city to another, as long as
they have permission and go through checkpoints.' " It turns out
that Karadzic's ideal for the new Sarajevo is the old Berlin. He accepts Zimmerman's description. " 'Yes,' he answered, 'our vision of
Sarajevo is like Berlin when the wall was still standing.' "[42] This is
ghastly, of course, but it is a logical conclusion of an absolutism of
the particular. The city held up as a horrific example of Soviet totalitarianism in action—Berlin divided by a wall—becomes the ex-
emplar for architects of the new ethnoculturalist nationalism: we
must build walls to separate different peoples because there is no
way they can live and work together civically. All of this gives one
a queasy sensation, as if one is in the presence of a return of the
repressed.

Those who fear forms of nationalism that feed on hatred of
ways of life have good grounds. But they go too far in claiming that
this is *always* the direction nationalism tends to take; therefore, the
sooner we have done with nationalist aspirations and identifications,

the better. But much of the new nationalism of 1989 involved remarkable outbursts of civic energy from long-suppressed peoples,
and the language in which these new citizens spoke was in and
through a civic rhetoric that tapped universal as well as particular
claims and concerns. The independence movements in the Baltic
states, Solidarity in Poland, Civic Forum in Czechoslovakia (before
the division into the Czech and Slovak Republics), among others,
protested their domination by the Soviet Union, first, because this
domination violated principles of self-determination embedded in
international law and widely shared understandings and customs
and, second, because it trampled on basic human rights, including
the right to participate in, and help to choose, a way of life.

Such appeals are at once universal and particular, tapping old
identities but energizing new political recognitions. Although this
is a story in the making, peoples who proclaim their devotion to
human rights as a universal principle can be held accountable, and
will hold themselves accountable, in ways rapacious, nationalistic de-
stroyers, who scoff at such niceties, cannot. This middle way—once
again as an alternative to warring racial and ethnic groupings or the
homogenized stability of efficiently managed imperialism—seems
to me the only possible course that respects claims to self-determination yet holds forth the prospect of a painfully attained and perhaps, for that very reason, even more deeply cherished civic order
based on universal principles of recognition.

Perhaps a concrete example of this delicate balancing act would
be helpful. I rely on press reports of Pope John Paul II's visit to the
Baltic States in September, 1993. The situation in Lithuania was particularly delicate for John Paul because "Polish nationalists for their
part have tried to exploit the alleged mistreatment of the 300,000
strong Polish minority in Lithuania." Thus, "the Pope had to be
very careful not to offend Lithuanian sensibilities," he being not
only the Pope but a Pole associated with Polish aspirations to self-
determination. It is worth reminding the reader that much of the
current Lithuania was once part of Poland. The Lithuanian capital,
Vilnius, is Poland's "Wilno," dear to the heart of Poles everywhere,
in part because it is the home of Adam Mickiewicz, the greatest
Polish poet. But John Paul, while acknowledging the love Poles have

for that particular place, used the Lithuanian name "Vilnius" and not the Polish "Wilno" throughout his pastoral visit, including the one time he spoke Polish—when he delivered mass in the main Polish-language church in Vilnius. For the rest of his visit, "the Pope spoke . . . Lithuanian which he had learnt for the occasion" and "this made a tremendously positive impression on the Lithuanians." The Poles "were not so pleased, but coming from the Pope they had to accept it. The Pope exhorted the Poles to identify fully with Lithuania, and not to dwell on the past—by which he meant not to endlessly recall the time when Vilnius was part of Poland."[43] This wonderful account shows the ways in which ethical space can be created or expanded for a form of civic identification *sans* irredentist or chauvinistic aspirations. One might say that eternal vigilance is the price of civic moderation.

Take a powerful example from the new South Africa as reported by a theologian and pastor, John W. deGruchy, a longtime foe of the apartheid system. In a piece called "Waving the Flag," deGruchy begins by telling us that he "never thought I would be seduced by civil religion. After all, part of the struggle against apartheid was against the civil religion of the Afrikaner nationalism that gave it birth." He then asks us to imagine his feelings of confusion as he unashamedly applauds "the civil religion of the new South Africa and experiences deep feelings of patriotism welling up in my soul." Now, as deGruchy continues, he has a "flag on my desk, a flag in the kitchen, a flag pinned to my pocket." But he knows there are limits: the fear of idolatry, warnings against making gods "in our own national image." For that reason, the flag of the new South Africa will not go into the sanctuary. "It is painful to do this—we would so much like to bring it in. But we need to do this to keep ourselves in check. The temptation of conflating civil religion with revelation has to be resisted."[44] This is an example—a powerful example—of how those formed in the Christian tradition are (rightly) drawn toward the civic goods embodied in a particular order, or the promise of such goods, but who must, at the same time, refuse any moves, however tempting and apparently innocent, to forge too tight an identity between their religious commitments and their national loyalties.

This brings me back to the claims of sovereignty and self-determination. Post-Nuremberg, such claims cannot trump all other claims in any instance of conflict. The issue of crimes against humanity and human rights has been a shaping force in the world arena and will continue to be such. Human rights may be a weak reed against coercive force, but it is often the only weapon beleaguered peoples have, and it offers a lever others can use to enforce the notion that geopolitical and cultural definitions of nationhood must, at this time in history, be open to chastening by universal principles. Of course, the Church has always advocated such chastening. But as we enter the twenty-first century, a bevy of international associations promulgates and nurtures this conviction as well. At the same time, the plurality of cultures is irreducible. A world of many nations, each with its own particular marks of identity, reminds us that we are not alone and that we cannot and ought not make the world "one" by cruelly obliterating diverse ways of life. Remember Václav Havel's arguments against the insidious nature of Communist universalism for its drive to "make everything the same," thereby producing a "vast shroud of uniformity." No, we are not the same. But we do share a capacity for identification with the idea of a plural political body; we all require self-dignity; we all yearn for a decent life for ourselves and our children.

This latter universalism is as different from the false universalism Havel denounces as the night is from the day. But there is a false pluralism as well. In the words of John Paul, "a falsely united multinational society [the Soviet Empire] must not be succeeded by one falsely diversified." (Here the Pope refers to the "racist pretensions and evil forms of nationalism.")[45] A universalism that sustains respect for difference is a universalism aware of our human need for concrete reference groups in order to attain and to sustain individuality and identity. As a version of national identity, the form of membership I here commend softens but does not negate altogether the idea of sovereignty. The alternative to strong theories of sovereignty that place duty and loyalty to the nation-state above all other duties and loyalties is "sovereignty . . . in the service of the people," in the words of the U.S. Bishops.[46] And their idea of sovereignty, remember, is filtered through the prism of subsidiarity which holds that the state exists to serve civil society and its many, overlapping, autonomous bodies and institutions. John Paul has elaborated an alternative to statist versions of sovereignty. In words I noted above, he argued, remember, that: "The state is firmly sovereign when it governs society and also serves the common good of society and allows the nation to realize its own subjectivity, its own identity."[47] This gestures toward a dialogical rather than monological political ideal. For various loci of human social existence are protected and served. Mind you, this isn't an argument for group rights, as multiculturalists usually talk about them, but for institutional integrity and autonomy. No group has a claim on protecting some romantic notion of the purity of its identity. But peoples do have legitimate claims that their social institutions—families, churches, solidaristic associations—be protected and recognized. This ideal offers a strong alternative to the cruelty and torment of a rapacious and narrow nationalism, on the one hand, and a watery universalism or impositional empire that either cannot inspire or else cruelly commands people's loyalties, on the other. This is surely what Václav Havel proposes when he writes of a politics of civic self-determination as a form of "practical morality . . . [sustained by] humanly measured care for our fellow human beings." Scoring the "arrogant anthropocentrism of modern man," an arrogance that attains at least one point of political culmination in triumphalist accounts of sovereignty and nationalism, Havel opts for limited ideals of identity and responsibility.[48] Politics, on this account, has to do with tending to one's particular home and its place in the wider world in which one gets one's bearings.

We live in a dangerous time, a time in which the forces of a new ethnoculturalist nationalism have taken shape in terrible ways. And, we live in an exciting time, a time in which the forces of a new birth of freedom have taken shape in tender ways.[49] In a powerful book alerting us to the many forms of the darker side of the "new nationalism," Michael Ignatieff shows us that it can look as menacing and behave as horribly as the term "ethnic cleansing" suggests, a new name for a very old phenomenon.[50] It can also creep up on cat's paws in the form of sad little tales of past injustice coupled with a no doubt unrealistic but very human desire for reparation, for putting things right somehow. We know the big stories of the shelling of cities, massacres, the breaking up of old multiethnic enclaves and ways of life. Writing of the "ethnically cleansed microstates that have taken the place of Yugoslavia" (and which the Dayton Accords more or less officially legitimated, presumably because no alternative was in sight), Ignatieff writes: "Ethnic apartheid may be an abomination, but for the more than two million refugees who have fled or been driven from their homes, apartheid is the only guarantee of safety they are prepared to trust."

This holds for aggressors and victims alike, for during the course of the Bosnian War, who was tormenter and who tormented shifted from week to week. Although the Serbs surely bear the major responsibility for the disaster in the Balkans, they are not solely responsible. The West, too, must take its fair share of blame. Ignatieff notes: "For the West failed to save Sarajevo, where Muslim, Croat, and Serb lived together in peace for centuries. It is asking the impossible to believe that ordinary people will trickle back to the multi-ethnic villages they have left behind, simply in order to vindicate our liberal principles." What Ignatieff tries to get the reader, perhaps dipping into his book in the comfort of an office or a soft reading chair in a den, to grasp is fear: the fear everywhere at work in struggles over the new nationalism, whether in the Balkans, Germany, Ukraine, Quebec, Kurdistan, or Northern Ireland, the sites that form the basis of his political journey. "There is one type of fear more devastating in its impact than any other: the systematic fear that arises when a state begins to collapse. Ethnic hatred is the result of the terror that arises when legitimate authority disintegrates." That all-pervasive fear is unknown to us in contemporary Western democracies in its primordial, most overwhelming form. But it is no stranger to many of our fellow human beings.

Ignatieff is not out to demonize nationalism. He recognizes, as all serious scholars of the subject must, the historically close connection between nationalism and democracy. "Nationalism, after all, is the doctrine that a people have a right to rule themselves, and that sovereignty reposes in them alone," he writes. The tragedy for the Balkans, then, has been that when democracy at last became possible, "the only language that existed to mobilize people into a shared civic project was the rhetoric of ethnic difference. Any possibility of a civic, as opposed to ethnic, democracy had been strangled at birth by the Communist regime." For in Tito's Yugoslavia there were no competing political parties, no independent loci of social and political life—the divisions were based on ethnicity alone, with the *apparat* perched on top holding everything in dictatorial order. People had no experience of democratic contestation in and through the category of civic membership. What existed in the old Yugoslavia was "manipulated plebiscitary democracy that ratifies one-man rule."

Ignatieff wants to disabuse us of a certain sort of liberal prejudice: the notion that what we see in the Balkans, or Northern Ireland, or elsewhere is an outburst of atavistic irrationalism. Rather, he situates us in complex social and political contexts, helping us to understand how and why and when people are driven to extremes of ethnic identification and contestation, even as he is horrified at the result. He reminds us of just how important national belonging really is and how it has come about that nation-states remain the dominant form of constituting and maintaining political bodies, for better or for worse. He suggests it is a bit of both. "It is only too apparent that cosmopolitanism is the privilege of those who can take a secure nation-state for granted," he notes provocatively. For cosmopolitanism, a blithe "post-nationalist spirit," depends, in ways its advocates and practitioners often refuse to recognize, "on the capacity of nation-states to provide security and civility for their citizens."

Ignatieff's is a vivid and sad journey. He takes us into the heart of fraught and fractured situations. He never adopts a stance of superior Western smugness toward those he interviews, encounters, sups and drinks with. We hear voices and see faces. For example, we hear a skinhead in the old East Germany (where, by the way, the most virulent forms of anti-foreign sentiment have broken out, not in the old West Germany with its nearly half century of democratic civic life). Ignatieff's interviews with "Leo," who embodies contemporary "skin culture," is filled up by Leo's talk, at once rageful and riddled with pathos. "If you see the world from his point of view," Ignatieff writes, "he comes from the only country in Europe that isn't allowed to feel good about itself." Germany is still required to atone for its sins. But young men like Leo were born well after the Third Reich and they are tired, apparently, of bearing the stigma of "Germanness." Perhaps Leo, then, is an example of what happens when a country "loses peaceful ways of being proud about itself, when the language of national pride is forced underground, when patriotism is hijacked by criminals." For Leo, "This isn't home, this is just misery." And out of that darkness of misery he lashes out.

Ukraine, Quebec, Kurdistan—we follow Ignatieff on his sober quest. The fears of his respondents come alive for us. The great tragedy, he concludes, is that ethnic nationalism, as a quest for sure and certain identity, must fail because it does not allow people to be truly themselves. They must sink their individuality into that of the group. It becomes an ethnic crime to fall in love and to marry outside the group. It becomes an ethnic crime to think in and through categories other than ethnicity. Nationalism, Ignatieff hastens to assure us, is not what is wrong with the world: "Every people must have a home, every such hunger must be assuaged." What is wrong is the "kind of nation, the kind of homeland that nationalists want to create and the means they use to seek their ends." If hatred of others is necessary in order to achieve your own group solidarity, you are on the road to bitter disappointment and in thrall to a likely cycle of recrimination and revenge. Ignatieff concludes:

> I began the journey as a liberal and I end as one, but I cannot help thinking that liberal civilization—the rule of laws, not men, of argument in place of force, of compromise in place of violence—runs deeply against the human grain and is achieved and sustained only by the most unremitting struggle against human nature. The liberal virtues—tolerance, compromise, reason—remain as valuable as ever, but they cannot be preached to those who are mad with fear or mad with vengeance.

That is Ignatieff's sober lesson for us, here in the waning years of the twentieth century. To those who preach wholly abstract sermons about peace and harmony and goodwill, Ignatieff would probably say: "Grow up. What we must come to realize is that nationalism is the chief political passion and force as we enter the twenty-first century. How will those in the stable and privileged West respond? With moral superiority and more preachments or with a tough-minded preparedness to engage in order, just perhaps, to help those who seek and need our help to arrive at least at those conditions of minimal safety from depradation that alone might help them to learn or to relearn the lessons of tolerance and moderation."

Sometimes, as I suggested above, the new nationalism is a story in miniature. Consider the fate of Karlovy Vary, also known as Karlsbad, the *belle époque* spa famous in literature, frequented by the likes of Nietzsche, Freud, and, in an earlier generation, Goethe. Karlovy Vary is in the Sudetenland, "a region once home to 65,000 Jews, 800,000 Czechs, and three million Germans."[51] When the Germans annexed the Sudetenland, they sent the Jewish population packing. Next the "Czechs eliminated Germans. Eduard Beneš, the pre-Communist post-war president, decreed their expulsion in 1945. At Potsdam, the Allies approved. As Germans fled toward Bavaria, Czechs took revenge. They murdered 40,000 Germans; many died at the end of a rope."

This episode was long-buried in the Communist deep freeze. But since 1989, "the expulsion has become a national nettle. . . . Czechs know that every Sudeten German wasn't guilty of Hitler's crimes." Oskar Schindler, by the way, was a Sudeten German. Although President Havel condemned the Sudeten expulsion, the Czech regime, as of 1994, wanted to keep the episode closed. In the meantime, children of Jewish and German victims of expulsion and murder are seeking, one by one, the return of their family houses. These are people with real names and faces, and quite specific and—in the grand scale of things—small stories and claims. Each is heartbreaking. The current policy permits Jewish families with claims to regain their houses; but German families cannot. The German descendants do not understand why their troubles count for nothing. One says, "My only crime was that for 800 years my ancestors lived in that place." They want repeal of the 1945 expulsion decree. They want a chance to get their property back. They want to return to their homeland, not just homes in Karlovy Vary but villages long emptied—ethnically cleansed—of their kind. But this will not happen.

Not every wrong can be righted. Not every injustice can be assuaged. Perhaps, at this juncture, Hannah Arendt's insistence that forgiveness is the greatest contribution of Jesus of Nazareth to politics should be noted. Perhaps there is nothing left for the expelled and expropriated people of German descent to do but to forgive. This gesture is made possible, in part, by President Havel's recognition of the past injustice they suffered. But forgiveness from the side of the aggrieved is more difficult—difficult but necessary in order to spur deeper soul-searching and recognition by the "other side." Forgiveness is the most difficult thing of all, of course, but it may be the the only way to forestall quaffing the bitter brew of injustice suffered and recompense sought even unto future generations. The nationalist principle does not take us very far at this point; it can only deepen rage, not sustain reconciliation. Forgiveness, I fear, may be a possibility utterly eclipsed by the new nationalism, whether writ large or small. We should all grow more fearful if I am right.

Epilogue

IS THERE ROOM FOR FORGIVENESS
IN INTERNATIONAL POLITICS?

SOMETIMES IT PAYS to take a bit longer than one should to revise lectures for publication. As I was putting the finishing touches on the text above, the *New York Times* reported a follow-up to the story about the Sudetenland, detailing the ways in which Germany will apologize for its invasion of the former Czechoslovakia and the Czechs, in turn, "will express regrets for the postwar expulsion of millions of Sudeten Germans. . . . "[52] The Germans apologize for Nazi "policies of violence." The Czechs express regret that their expulsions "caused suffering and injustice to innocent people." But, of course, things are not made right in the eyes of those who suffered most. The story indicates that an organization of Sudeten Germans, a "powerful political lobby in Bavaria," takes strong exception to the agreement that has been hammered out because "it provides them with neither a claim to compensation nor a right to return to expropriated properties." As well, the *Times* tells us, the agreement "seems likely to incense many Czechs because it apologizes for events that many view as an appropriate reaction to Nazi occupation."

No doubt true. Hardliners are already standing in queue waiting for an opportunity to erupt. But still, these small steps, each of which acknowledges violation of "elementary, humanitarian principles" should not be sneezed at altogether. As I already argued, reparation and compensation and return are not in the cards. But acknowledgment and recognition of injustice is forthcoming. Maybe there is a political version of forgiveness that must, not all of the time but most of the time, step back from full reconciliation and certainly from absolution. There are no sacraments, no blessings, no benedictions in politics. Thinking politically, one might ask what sorts of deeds warrant the solemn drama of forgiveness of a sort related to, yet different from, the different acts that constitute a personal redemption narrative.

When Hannah Arendt called forgiveness the greatest political contribution of Jesus of Nazareth to politics, she didn't have in mind a single political figure saying, "Can you forgive me?" Rather, she was gesturing toward a way to break repetitive cycles of vengeance, to forestall the often deadly playing out of horrible deeds done and equally horrible retribution sought. Forgiveness, an unexpected act, disrupts automatic processes and opens a space for something new to begin: for the possibility that bloody deeds will not haunt generation upon generation in perpetuity. Although individual acts of forgiveness—one human being to another—most often take place outside the full glare of publicity, there are others that are noteworthy for the public message they bear. I think here of Pope John Paul II, who barely survived an assassin's bullets, uttering his first public words from his hospital bed to his "brother, whom I have sincerely forgiven," words that preceded his extraordinary visit to his brother and would-be killer in jail once he was up and about. The Pope was practicing what some have called the "craft" of forgiveness and, in so doing, displaying to the world the ways in which forgiveness is not primarily about a singular moment but about an enactment within a particular way of life.

But it would be odd to call John Paul's act of forgiveness a political intervention per se, although it was an undeniably powerful moment, one seared into the memory and locked in the hearts of all who witnessed it, even from afar and through the medium of television news. To be sure, there might have been political consequences: the Pope's words and actions might have quieted the turbulent hearts of many believers who sought revenge for his near-murder. But I doubt this is quite what Arendt had in mind. She was more concerned with interrupting the flow of events that seem to be on automatic pilot when mass murder, acts of retribution, then more killing become the "way we do things here," so to speak. Within the frame of such broad-based events driven by desperate political purpose, *individuals* who are shaped by the practice of forgiveness should practice what they believe or preach. But an individual cannot from himself or herself stem the rushing tide of violence—or, such moments will be quite rare. Can there, then, be authentic acts of political forgiveness? Who forgives whom and for what? Remember: forgiveness isn't a one-way street. It implies a relationship, or requires a transitive dimension, because it is not primarily about self-exculpation but about the creation of a new relationship or the restoration of one that has been broken and torn by violence.

Here one confronts head-on the sheer weight of history—its denseness and thickness. People are often fond of citing Santayana's claim that those who don't know their history are doomed to repeat it. The reverse seems more true, namely, that those who know their history perhaps too well are doomed to repetition. Perhaps a certain amount of 'knowing forgetting' is necessary in order to get out of the rut of repetition. By 'knowing forgetting' I have in mind a way to release present-day actors from the full burden of the past in order that they not be weighed down by it utterly. Forgetting, in this instance, doesn't mean falling into radical present-mindedness and the delusion that the past counts for nothing; rather, one assesses and judges just what the past counts for in the present, how much it should frame, shape, even determine present events.

Too often when forgiveness is mentioned, it is translated into a bland evocation of nonjudgmentalness of the sort that means I can't say anything at all about anybody else's behavior and words. But if this is the tack one takes, forgiveness is altogether unnecessary. There can never be anything to forgive if no real wrong has been suffered, no real sin committed, no evil deed perpetrated.

Forgiveness is a strenuous discipline, for it aims at the restoration of a relationship when a relationship has been broken; it requires acknowledgment of wrongs perpetrated or wrongly suffered. Forgiveness in public or political life must also involve the painful recognition of the limits to forgiveness itself, if what one seeks is expiation or a full accounting. There are wrongs suffered that can never be put right; indeed, this latter recognition is itself a central feature of an overall structure of political forgiveness, or so I want to suggest. There are many examples one might point to. How does a culture expiate for the Holocaust? For slavery? Wrongs that cannot be righted must, nonetheless, be acknowledged. Part of that acknowledgment will consist in a knowing and explicit articulation of the terrible fact that full expiation is impossible. This is *not* forgetting as a kind of collective amnesia; rather, it is an explicit recognition of the full scope of a given horror and the inability of a subsequent generation to put things right. The events stand. Acknowledgment of these events is required by those most directly implicated, and even by those not so directly implicated who, perhaps, stood by and did nothing. But, unless one undertakes a course of retribution, the repetition of violence perpetrated must stop even as the remembrance of past violence must go forward in all its fullness, all its detail. In fact, the sheer recitation of events counts as an ongoing indictment tethered to a tragic recognition that some wrongs cannot be righted.

This must have been what Arendt had in mind, at least in part. In her controversial book, *Eichmann in Jerusalem,* she justifies the hanging of Adolph Eichmann because he had perpetrated terrible crimes against humanity "on the body of the Jewish people," but she did so in full recognition that no scale of justice had thereby been put right and that hanging every known Nazi war criminal would not do that.[53] She also knew that young Germans could not be held accountable for what occurred. But they were obliged to remember in order that they could be free to act in other ways. This is 'knowing forgetting', then: recollection of the past, yes, but not being so wholly defined by it that one's options are either to be victim or executioner, in Albert Camus's memorable phrase. Here is one concrete and no doubt modest example of the dynamic I have in mind, although it does take place in the most difficult of all arenas for the dynamic of forgiveness and 'knowing forgetting' to play out—the realm of relations between peoples and states. But if forgiveness is to have real political sturdiness, it must be tested in many arenas. My example is drawn from Northern Ireland and its centuries-old troubled relationship with Great Britain. Irish Catholics in Northern Ireland have long been a tormented people, relegated to second-class citizenship in what they perceive to be part of their land. But Irish Catholics, relatively powerless in the overall balance of forces, have also been tormenters, as the history of IRA terrorism and death-dealing attests.

It is, therefore, significant, that on January 22, l995, Cardinal Cahal Daly of Armagh, Northern Ireland, publicly asked forgiveness from the people of Britain in a speech at Canterbury Cathedral, England, the home (as readers surely know) of the primate of the Church of England, the Archbishop of Canterbury. Cardinal Daly's words on that occasion are worth pondering:

> We Irish are sometimes said to be obsessively concerned with memories of the past. It is salutary, however, to recall that the faults we attribute to others can be a projection of faults within ourselves which we have not had the courage to confront. . . . What is certainly true is that we all need a healing of memories. . . . Healing of memories demands recognition of our own need for forgiveness; it requires repentance. The original biblical term for repentance, *metanoia,* is a strong word indicating the need for radical conversion, change of attitude, change of outlook, change of stance; and all this is costing and can be painful. The old word *contrition* expresses it well. . . . This healing, this conversion, this reciprocal giving and accepting of forgiveness are essential elements in the healing of relationships between our two islands and between our divided communities in Northern Ireland. . . . On this occasion . . . I wish to ask forgiveness from the people of this land for the wrongs and hurts inflicted by Irish people upon the people of this country on many occasions during that shared history, and particularly in the past 25 years. I believe that this reciprocal recognition of the need to forgive and to be forgiven is a necessary condition for proper Christian, and human, and indeed *political relationships* between our two islands in the future [emphasis mine].[54]

The Cardinal continued with words about starting "something new" and how frightful it would be to "slide back into violence." What he was saying and doing was avowedly political in the sense of drawing from the Gospel "conclusions which are relevant to our daily living as individuals and as a society. . . . " Reciprocal forgiveness and reconciliation were also offered by the Anglican primate of Ireland as well as the Archbishop of Canterbury himself. A question, then: is this form of forgiveness, to the extent that it is accessible and enactable, available only to communicants of a faith? The Cardinal suggests not when he addresses "human" and "political" relationships more generally. For many, certainly for international relations scholars, this is a hopelessly idealistic stance out of touch with tough realities. But the riposte might be that tough realities invite precisely this stance; indeed, they suggest it as a necessary part of a process of negotiation, reconciliation, starting something new. Of course, there is not yet peace in Northern Ireland. But I am convinced that words and deeds of tough-minded reconciliation and forgiveness are a part of that process. They provide a moral deposit on which future generations can draw in an effort not to slide back into recriminatory cycles.

Nothing I have said should be taken as an injunction to fiddle while Rome burns or pray as the Vandals storm the city. There are times when action is necessary in order to prevent a wrong from being committed. In daily life with those we love, the process of forgiveness is an enactment that is part of the very dailyness of existence: it makes the quotidian livable. But in the affairs of what used to be called men and states, these enactments are not and cannot be so ordinary and so direct. But that does not preclude 'knowing forgetting' and an interplay of justice and forgiveness altogether.[55] Over the past several years, the Japanese government has apologized to all those women still alive who were forced into prostitution as "comfort ladies" under Japanese dominion in World War II. This official act was preceded by public acknowledgment and recognition of the wrongs perpetrated upon the bodies of violated women by the thousands. Official recognition; some form of reparation; state-level apology. The scales are somewhat righted. It is such difficult and fragile achievements that politics and forgiveness, or the politics *of* forgiveness, is all about.

NOTES

My thanks to Raimo Väyrynen, Director of the Joan B. Kroc Institute for International Peace Studies, University of Notre Dame, for the invitation to deliver the 1996 Hesburgh Lectures, and to both him and his staff and colleagues for their generous hospitality during my visit to Notre Dame. Thanks also to Fred Dallmayr and Martha Merritt of the Notre Dame faculty for their perspicuous commentaries.

1. See, for example, my essay, "International Politics and Political Theory," in Ken Booth and Steven Smith, eds., *International Relations Theory Today* (Cambridge: Polity Press, 1995), pp. 263–278.

2. Alan James, *Sovereign Statehood: The Basis of International Society* (London: Allen and Unwin, 1986), p. 7. At points throughout this chapter I draw upon several earlier 'cuts' into the question of sovereignty, the most recent being "Rethinking Sovereignty," in Francis A. Beer and Robert Hariman, eds., *Post-Realism: The Rhetorical Turn in International Relations* (East Lansing: Michigan State University Press, 1996).

3. Hannah Arendt, *Men in Dark Times* (New York: Harcourt, Brace and World, 1968).

4. See, for example, Donna Warnock, "Patriarchy is a Killer: What People Concerned about Peace and Justice Should Know," in Pam McAllister, ed., *Reweaving the Web of Life* (Philadelphia: New World, 1982).

5. Václav Havel, "The Post-Communist Nightmare," *New York Review of Books*, May 27, 1993, p. 8.

6. Drawn from Wilson's third annual message to Congress as cited by David M. Kennedy in *Over Here: The First World War and American Society* (New York: Oxford University Press, 1980), p. 24. For a more complete recounting of these events, see the discussion in my book, *Women and War* (New York: Basic Books, 1987), pp. 113–120.

7. Reverend John Murray, "A Biblical Theological Study," in Jacob T. Hoogstra, ed., *The Sovereignty of God, or the Proceedings of the First American Calvinistic Conference* (Grand Rapids, Mich.: Zondervan Publishing House, 1939), pp. 25–44.

8. Carl Schmitt, *Political Theology: Four Chapters on the Concept of Sovereignty*, trans. George Schwab (Cambridge, Mass.: MIT Press, 1985), p. 36.

9. Jean Bodin, *Six Books of the Commonwealth*, trans. M. J. Tooley (New York: MacMillan, 1955), pp. 25–27, 28, 32.

10. Thomas Hobbes, *The Leviathan* (Baltimore: Penguin, 1968), esp. pp. 227, 236.

11. To be sure, they were working from, and appropriating to their own

purposes, a body of pre-statist sovereign theory penned by defenders of the papacy as the site of *plenitudo potestatis*, a plenitude, an untrammeled amplitude of power. Writes Antony Black: "Long before this period, Roman imperial doctrine had been used by national kings and territorial princes to justify the overriding of positive law, and a centralized system of legislation and appointment. Papal doctrine . . . supplied something of the more abstract . . . notion of sovereignty which was to be fully developed in the work of Bodin." Antony Black, *Monarchy and Community: Political Ideas in the Later Conciliar Controversy, 1430–1450* (Cambridge: Cambridge University Press, 1970), pp. 80–81.

12. Before Bodin and Hobbes had penned their classics, the peace of Augsburg (1555) had embedded the principle of *cujus regio–ejus religio* in treaty law applicable to German principalities. Luther had helped to unleash more than he knew, for here one finds set in motion a theory of sovereignty that assimilates confessional and political particularity. The full-blown dimensions of this political theology became more visible in seventeenth-century calls for holy wars, providentially enjoined. Following the excesses of Europe's so-called religious wars, the crusading ethos does not disappear; it regroups, taking shape as the popular bellicism and militarism of the nineteenth century, further feeding notions of sovereignty as a secular mimesis of God construed as Ultimate Law Giver whose commandments must be obeyed and whose power to judge is absolute and final. There is no appeal "beyond."

13. Perry Anderson, *Lineages of the Absolutist State* (London: NLB, 1974), pp. 20, 23, 26.

14. John Gerard Ruggie, "Continuity and Transformation in the World Polity," in Robert Keohane, ed., *Neorealism and its Critics* (New York: Columbia University Press, 1986), pp. 131–157, esp. p. 144.

15. Cited in Black, *Monarchy and Community*, p. 74. See also Walter Ullmann, "The Development of the Medieval Idea of Sovereignty," *English Historical Review* no. 250 (1949), pp. 1–33.

16. Charles E. Merriam, Jr., *History of the Theory of Sovereignty since Rousseau*, Studies in History, Economics and Public Law vol. 12, no. 4 (New York: Columbia University Press, 1900), pp. 33–35.

17. See Hendrik Spruyt, *The Sovereign State and Its Competitors* (Princeton, N.J.: Princeton University Press, 1994).

18. Cited in François Furet, *Interpreting the French Revolution*, trans. Elborg Forster (New York: Cambridge University Press, 1981), p. 53.

19. Arnold Brecht, "Sovereignty," in Hans Speier and Alfred Kahler, eds., *War in Our Time* (New York: W. W. Norton, 1939), p. 62.

20. F. H. Hinsley, *Sovereignty*, 2d ed. (Cambridge: Cambridge University Press, 1988), p. 17.

21. 2 Dallas 419, 454. The "one place" Wilson has in mind is, of course, the Preamble to the Constitution. The question before the Court in *Chisholm v. Georgia* was: May a citizen of one state sue another state in the federal courts? The answer: Sure. The result: Amendment XI to reverse the decision. Amendment XI reads: "The Judicial power of the United States shall not be construed

to extend to any suit in law or equity, commenced or prosecuted against one of the United States by Citizens of another State, or by Citizens or Subjects of any Foreign State."

22. 11 U.S. (7 Cranch) 116, 136.

23. 299 U.S. 304.

24. See Otto Gierke's difficult but valuable discussion in *Associations and Law: The Classical and Early Christian Stages*, ed. and trans. George Heiman (Toronto: University of Toronto Press, 1977), pp. 96–97.

25. Black, *Monarchy and Community*, p. 67.

26. For a full account see Jean Bethke Elshtain, *Public Man, Private Woman: Women in Social and Political Thought* (Princeton, N.J.: Princeton University Press, 1981, 2d ed., 1992).

27. Hannah Arendt, "What is Freedom?" in *Between Past and Future* (New York: Penguin Books, 1980), pp. 164–165. See also her *On Violence* (New York: Harcourt Brace Jovanovich, 1969), in which she makes the claim that the *Chisholm v. Georgia* case means sovereignty is unknown to the Constitution of the United States. As I have shown, this is just plain wrong. Arendt can make this point by ignoring all subsequent strong cases proclaiming sovereignty in the classical mold.

28. Adam Michnik, "Towards a Civil Society: Hopes for a Polish Democracy," *Times Literary Supplement,* February 19–25, 1988, pp. 198–199.

29. Havel has written of these matters in many places. The interested reader might just begin with his classic essay on "The Power and Powerlessness of Citizens" in pre-1989 Central Eastern Europe in Jan Vladislav, ed., *Václav Havel, or Living in Truth* (London: Faber and Faber, 1987).

30. From a homily at Jasna Góra in 1983 as cited in Timothy Garton Ash, *The Uses of Adversity: Essays on the Fate of Central Eastern Europe* (New York: Random House, 1989), p. 53.

31. Sir Isaiah Berlin, "Two Concepts of Nationalism," *New York Review of Books,* November 21, 1991, p. 20. See Jean Bethke Elshtain, "Nationalism and Self-Determination: The Bosnian Tragedy," in G. Scott Davis, ed., *Religion and Justice in the War Over Bosnia* (New York: Routledge, 1996), pp. 45–62.

32. Liah Greenfeld, *Nationalism: Five Roads to Modernity* (Cambridge, Mass.: Harvard University Press, 1992), pp. 487–488.

33. Havel, "The Post-Communist Nightmare."

34. Pope John XXIII, "Pacem in Terris," in *The Encyclicals and Other Messages of John XXIII* (Washington, D.C.: TPS Press, 1964), p. 347.

35. Ibid., p. 350.

36. George Orwell, "Notes on Nationalism," in *The Collected Essays, Journalism, and Letters of George Orwell,* ed. Sonia Orwell and Ian Angus (New York: Harvest, HBJ, 1968), vol. 3: pp. 362–363.

37. U.S. Bishops, "The Harvest of Peace is Sown in Justice," *Origins* 23, no. 26 (December 9, 1993), p. 458.

38. John Keane, "Democracy's Poisonous Fruit," *Times Literary Supplement,* August 21, 1992, p. 10.

39. Robert Coles, *The Political Life of Children* (Boston: Atlantic Monthly Press, 1986), pp. 60–63.

40. G. M. Tamas, "Old Enemies and New: A Philosophic Postscript to Nationalism," in *Studies in East European Thought* (Netherlands: Kluwer Academic Publishers, 1993), p. 120.

41. Ibid., p. 121.

42. Warren Zimmerman, "The Last Ambassador," *Foreign Affairs* 64, no. 2 (March / April 1995), p. 20.

43. I rely on Anatol Lieven's account, "The Pope's Balancing Act," *The Tablet*, September 18, 1993, pp. 1208–1209.

44. John W. deGruchy, "Waving the Flag," *Christian Century*, June 12–15, 1994, pp. 597–598.

45. "Pope Sees False Nationalism Tearing at Europe," *The Tablet*, December 4, 1993, p. 1599.

46. "The Harvest of Peace is Sown in Justice," p. 453.

47. Cited in Ash, *The Uses of Adversity*, p. 53.

48. These insights appear throughout Havel's work. The reader might want to consult both early and late essays. But see, especially, Václav Havel, *Disturbing the Peace* (New York: Alfred A. Knopf, 1990) and *Summer Meditations* (New York: Knopf, 1992).

49. Here, of course, my reference point is what Czechs call "the Tender Revolution," their nonviolent transition toward freedom and constitutionalism. In the West, this got called the "Velvet Revolution," but my Czech friends tell me "tender" is the better translation.

50. All cites are from Michael Ignatieff, *Blood and Belonging: Journeys into the New Nationalism* (New York: Farrar, Straus and Giroux, 1994).

51. All quotes are drawn from the story, "Czech Republic Fields Demands of Germans, Jews, for Lost Homes," *The Wall Street Journal*, July 15, 1994, pp. 1, 6.

52. Alan Crowell, "Germans and Czechs Agree To Pact on Wartime Abuses," *The New York Times*, December 12, 1996, p. A12.

53. Hannah Arendt, *Eichmann in Jerusalem* (New York: Penguin Books, 1977).

54. The text of this address in full can be found under the title, "Breakdown of the Cease-Fire," *Origins* 25, no. 35 (February 22, 1996), pp. 585–588.

55. This epilogue was written before I made a trip to South Africa, in August 1997. Were I writing the epilogue tody, material from this encounter would be incorporated. As it is, that must wait another day, for yet another essay or book.

COMMENTS

ETHICS AND THE LIMITS OF POLITICS
Comments on Elshtain
Fred Dallmayr

IN THESE WANING years of the century, it behooves all of us, especially the theoretically minded, to glance back to discover what lessons might be gleaned from the experiences of our age. What we thus behold in retrospect is a grim and forbidding landscape: a century littered with corpses, punctuated by global wars, genocide, gulags, and ethnic cleansing. In the midst of imposing scientific and technological advances and in the teeth of "development" on all sides, we are confronted with a spectacle of immense human agony and tragedy. Faced with this panorama, the temptation is great to drift into morbid pessimism, perhaps even into cynicism and despair. How can one still celebrate human decency and the vision of a humane order of things without appearing to shunt aside, and even to insult, the victims of history? How can one still speak of ethics—especially political ethics and, still more, an ethics of international politics—without seeming to indulge in pious sermonizing and a string of highmindedly empty platitudes? How can one still plausibly and believably address a morally wounded age? There are few voices in our time willing and able to address us on that level. In my view, Jean Elshtain is one of the few intellectuals in America who credibly can engage in a discourse linking ethics and politics.

What distinguishes and renders credible Elshtain's discourse is her unabashed complicity with her readers (and listeners). In talking about ethics, she does not occupy the high ground of moral abso-

lutism and a "preachy" self-righteousness, but prefers to place herself at the grassroots level, into the crucible of the "human predica-
ment" in our time. Differently phrased: her discourse does not talk
at people but rather *with* people, thereby being able to resonate with
human agonies and aspirations. Elshtain herself calls her attitude
"realistic"; but we should be careful to note the special kind of realism involved here. Her realism is not one which simply endorses
"the way things are," especially the way things are politically at
home and in the world. Rather, hers is a sober and chastened
humanism, an outlook which is tough-mindedly aware of both the
promises and the limitations and risks of politics. As one may note,
this outlook is akin to the one she ascribes to St. Augustine in one
of her recent books, *Augustine and the Limits of Politics*. As she
writes there, in an eloquent and memorable passage placed near the
end of her study:

> Now is the time to get sober and to remember what St. Augustine
> taught: . . . The earthly city is never free from the dangers of
> bloodshed, sedition, and war. A human being cannot even be cer-
> tain of "his own conduct on the morrow," let alone specify and
> adjudicate that of others in ways he or she foreordains. In this
> world of discontinuities and profound yearnings, of sometimes ter-
> rible necessities, a human being can yet strive to maintain or to
> create an order that approximates justice, to prevent the worst from
> happening, and to resist the seductive lure of imperial grandiosity.[1]

It is good and proper, in my view, to keep her *Augustine* study
in mind when reflecting on Elshtain's Hesburgh Lectures. The title
of her lectures, of course—"New Wine and Old Bottles"—bristles
with biblical allusions, conjuring up the quandary of the embroil-
ment of the "old" and the "new." When talking about a certain complicity between her books and her readers, it is well to note
the complex character of this complicity, which is far removed
from chummy coziness or a trendy desire for relevance. Although
very much our contemporary, Elshtain does not aim to be avant-
gardist—or, at least, her avant-gardism curiously resonates both
with distant portents and with lingering traces and memories.
Prominent among these memories is the legacy of St. Augustine,

whose teachings, in her treatment, emerge as a "new wine" which may yet stir a dissolute and complacent age to greater sobriety and critical self-awareness. Thus, in conversing with her readers and listeners, Elshtain is not loath to char or unsettle late-modern conceits. When contemporary avant-gardist intellectuals attack "a triumphalistic, logocentric metanarrative" and indict "the Western tradition or Euro-centrism," she observes at one point, "I am unsure they know what they are talking about when the claim is that sweeping." A main reason for her uneasiness is the multidimensionality or internal diversity of "the Western tradition" which, in some ways, has always lived in protest against itself. Among others, Augustine has been such an internal protester, and he could well serve as "an ally in critiques" of a misguided logocentrism—provided the conceit of avant-gardism is discarded. As matters stand, however, the African bishop "remains an irritant to us bold postmoderns who believe we are daring to go where no human being has gone before. He was there before us."[2]

Elshtain's distance from a "bold" or avant-gardist type of postmodernism is evident both in the content and in the style of her arguments. Disenchanted with rational transparency, recent attacks on "logocentrism" have sometimes encouraged a radical shift from meaning to writing or textuality—a textuality occasionally portrayed as utterly opaque and self-enclosed, ensconced in (what some have called) the "prison-house of language." Although an accomplished stylist and well versed in the exigencies of writing, Elshtain does not share in this vaunted "boldness." Finely crafted, her texts are never windowless but remain porously open to real-life experience, thus allowing the "discontinuities and profound yearnings" of our age as well as the torments of the human heart to shine through in language. With regard to Augustine, Elshtain refuses the lure both of radical distantiation and of a deconstructive reading reducing the meaning of his teachings to the dry bones of ancient texts. As she notes in her study on the bishop: "To be unmoved by *The Confessions*, to see in them only feed for the clinical grinder; only evidence of a solidification of the triumph of Western logocentricism, is to have a heart of stone and a head of brick."[3] The same experiential openness, the same resonance with real-life agonies is

evident in her Hesburgh Lectures, which clearly are addressed not
solely to international relations experts but more broadly to partici-
pants in the multiple struggles of our time. Both in the substance
and the style of her presentation, Elshtain does not curry the favor
of "value-neutral" social scientists or of disengaged onlookers or
spectators of the human drama. As she states in her lectures, even
Max Weber—who is credited with having invented the phrase—was
keenly aware of the practical flaw of value-neutrality. As a mature
and responsible citizen, Weber "made the observation a long time
ago that if you have a policy of pure interest severed from ethics,
things get brutal and opportunistic too easily."

   In terms of ethical theory, her lectures seek to steer a course between "pure" interest and obligation, or rather a course that would
mediate between concrete sensibility and duty, between finite
human contexts and infinite demands. As indicated before, Elshtain
is not given to high-flown doctrines and certainly not to millenar-
ian blueprints or panaceas pledging to end or "resolve" the human
drama. In her lectures, she refuses the temptation to "blanket the
world of international politics with ethical normativity." More
pointedly, she distances herself from hopes to "enforce an international Kantianism" around the globe—partly because of their impossibility (given the gulf between duty and interest), partly because
of their streamlining coerciveness. In the preface to her *Augustine*
study, she inserts a "confession" of her own by reporting that, in
earlier years, she had taken "intensive crash courses" on Kant and
had emerged "not only unconvinced but unmoved" (the air seeming "awfully thin up there"). She also confesses her early affection
for Albert Camus—still one of her favorite writers—in whom she
found "an eloquent ally in my repudiation of rationalistic triumphalism" and the repulsive politics of "logical deliriums." In the
middle of her book, Elshtain comments on a lecture given by Camus
at the end of World War II (at Columbia University) where Camus
had highlighted the "human crisis" of our time by evoking some
of the ghastly episodes of brutality from which Europe had just
emerged. Attributing the crisis chiefly to the cult of technical ef-
ficiency and ideological abstraction, Camus then stated that "this is
why man in Europe today experiences only solitude and silence; for

he cannot communicate with his fellows in terms of [concrete] values common to all." Taking her cues from that lecture, Elshtain counters both a narrow utilitarianism (predicated on interest) and an abstract normativism by embracing an ethics of care attending to "a fragile human commonality that is in danger of being lost and that must be struggled for and reaffirmed."[4]

The chief aim of her Hesburgh Lectures is to articulate the linkage between ethics and politics, particularly international politics, in our contemporary global context. In a way, this articulation provides a commentary on, and perhaps a qualification of, a phrase used in the title of her *Augustine* book: the phrase "the limits of politics." As emerges in the course of her lectures, these "limits" are not merely external boundaries or delimitations, within whose perimeters "politics" could remain unchallenged. Construed not in terms of abstract rules but of lived engagement, ethics for Elshtain does not impinge on politics from the outside, but rather inhabits it throughout, though without being fully submerged. Proceeding in this manner, her lectures intimate the contours of a difficult mutual entwinement, equally removed from segregation and coincidence. As she states herself, the main goal of her lectures is to "draw the ethical and the political into a complex relationship with one another"—a relationship involving not "two meticulously demarcated spheres that must be delicately pushed together, rather like porcupines greeting one another," but rather two distinct activities which are yet "mutually constitutive." As one may note, this view of differential entwinement is akin to the relation between other key categories in Elshtain's thought, especially those of public and private, self and other. As she writes in another recent study, *Democracy on Trial,* the traditional male usurpation of the public domain made it imperative and defensible at one point "to politicize and to challenge the notion of separate spheres—the male public world and the female private world." However, this challenge by no means vindicated the complete fusion of spheres, according to the slogan "the personal is political" (or the private is public). Her study in this connection cites with approval the Czech novelist Milan Kundera who, in an interview in 1984, insisted on a "magic border" between intimate life and public life "that can't be crossed with impunity."[5]

Taken with the preceding caveats, the Hesburgh Lectures can indeed be read as elaborations on the limits of politics, where politics emerges as an important and unrelinquishable, yet not wholly autonomous or self-constituted sphere. Seen from this angle, her argument pits itself both against a reckless inflation and a precipitous erasure or displacement of politics. Both temptations have been powerful in our century, although the former has wreaked more obvious havoc than the latter. In various guises, our century has been savaged and nearly devastated by a "limitless" politics, a politics of absolute or unlimited power vested in regimes which we commonly and appropriately call "totalitarian." Under the auspices of both fascism and Stalinist communism, society and human life were placed in the straitjacket of a seemingly self-contained politics, a politics without windows, without breathing space or room for "otherness." With the end of the Cold War, we have witnessed the end of this virulent and nightmarish kind of totalitarianism, although to be sure, totalizing ambitions (in the form of ethnic or religious fundamentalism) have by no means subsided. In a radical reversal of trends, the demise of the Cold War has ushered in the triumphant upsurge of market liberalism or economic liberalization, now on a global scale. Buttressed by the ongoing information revolution and the expanding reach of multinational corporations, this market liberalism sometimes proclaims not only the end of the nation-state (especially in weaker countries), but the end of politics as such or at least its near effacement in favor of consumerism and private profit-seeking. As it happens, both temptations of our century have been vigorously denounced by Hannah Arendt, with Camus one of Elshtain's favorite authors. While her study of totalitarianism critiqued political megalomania, Arendt's book *The Human Condition* bemoaned the progressive emaciation of the *vita activa* in favor of depoliticized programs and private self-indulgence.[6]

Together with Hannah Arendt, Elshtain champions the path of a limited but robust public life, a path which respects both the legitimate ends of politics and its elusive horizons and blank spaces—including those transempirical moments which can never be fully managed or controlled by (human) power. In her presentation, the legitimate end of politics is the establishment of a certain kind of order and the pursuit or cultivation of some form of the common good shareable by a public community. This pursuit, however, becomes illegitimate when "order" turns into a prison cell or concentration camp and when the "common good" is instrumentalized into a weapon to beat down the non-common or uncommon, that is, alternative visions of the good. In the Hesburgh Lectures, this middle path is illustrated and fleshed out through the discussion of two prominent themes in contemporary international politics and political theory: those of sovereignty and of nationalism or the nation-state. Although both are closely interrelated, it may be well to reflect and comment on the two topics in turn.

In many ways, the idea of sovereignty demarcates a crucial watershed separating modern from pre-modern political life and thought. Elshtain's lectures offer an erudite account of the historical emergence of the idea, pointing to such contributing factors as the splintering of the medieval order, the rapaciousness of religious wars, and the incorporation (or "reception") of such Roman-law concepts as "legal subjectivity" and *imperium*. Roman-law *imperium*, she notes, contrasted with the chaotic particularism of feudal times, while the concept of legal subjectivity (anchored in property rights) buttressed in turn the "exclusive authority over territorial space." The lectures also allude to deeper, more recessed theological underpinnings of the modern idea: particularly the post-Occamite reconstruction of the *imago Dei* in terms of untrammeled sovereign lordship. Regarding the historical unfolding of the idea in modern political thought, proper attention is given to the argumentative line leading from Bodin over Hobbes to Rousseau and the celebration of popular sovereignty. (An interesting aside in this connection are the comments on American constitutionalism, demonstrating the sly but firm insinuation of the idea of sovereignty into the trajectory of judicial review.) Turning to more recent times, Elshtain ponders the growing contestation and problematicization of sovereignty under the combined impact of both political developments (like globalization) and internal-philosophical reassessments. Prominent in the latter domain is Hannah Arendt's famous indictment of political sovereignty—an indictment expressed on numerous occasions, especially in her statements that the linkage of freedom with

sovereignty may well be "the most pernicious and dangerous consequence of the political equation of freedom and free will" and
that, consequently, if men "wish to be free, it is precisely sovereignty
they must renounce."[7]

While generally applauding Arendt's sentiments, Elshtain is hesi-
tant to embrace her wholesale indictment of sovereignty, at least in
the absence of further elaborations attentive to the immense complexity of our contemporary situation. Although recognizing the
homogenizing and often repressive effects of sovereignty in domestic affairs, Elshtain is equally apprehensive of the simple effacement
of sovereignty in favor of a triumphant globalism—which in effect
merely equals superpower hegemony. Her lectures point to the
yearning for "a universal order, a new and better *pax Romana*"
(read: *pax Americana*) and to the attempt to construct a "universal
political regime" that would guarantee peace by stripping individual
countries of sovereign prerogatives. Unimpressed by "one world"
rhetoric, Elshtain queries whether such globalism would not be the
harbinger of "a tyranny of a sort hitherto unknown, even in the
darkest moments of mid-twentieth-century totalitarianism," of a
"concentration of power awesome and terrifying to behold." Turning to events in Eastern Europe, she stresses the legitimacy of national independence movements in countries long buried under a
"vast shroud of uniformity." For leaders like Václav Havel and Lech
Wałęsa, the rhetoric of universal order was bound to appear as a
"recipe for hegemony"; having just emerged from domination and
freshly tasting the fruits of independence, such people were "unlikely to be persuaded by attacks on sovereignty as run-amok particularism." Elshtain's comments could be extended from Eastern
Europe to the large number of "Third World" countries erstwhile
under colonial domination and still struggling against pressures of
neocolonialism. In the words of Chandra Muzaffer, the dedicated
Malaysian champion of the legitimate (though not unbounded)
rights of Third World countries today:

> As societies the world over are globalized, as local economics and
> local cultures are siphoned into structures and systems that are con-
> trolled to a large degree by the centers of power in the West, they

will have to devise schemes and strategies which would enable them to protect their integrity and identity. In other words, while there may be aspects of globalization which are positive and therefore worth absorbing, there will also be elements of globalization that are negative and therefore worth resisting. . . . [T]he best way of resisting the negative dimensions of globalization is by fortifying what is valuable and virtuous in one's own religion, culture and tradition.[8]

As it seems to me, Muzaffer's statement points to a plausible— perhaps the only plausible—restraint on state sovereignty, both at home and internationally. Translated into another idiom, the reference to "religion, culture and tradition" can be read as an allusion to "civil society," that is, the multidimensional fabric of social life which is neither wholly private nor completely public or politicized. In her lectures, Elshtain repeatedly pays tribute to civil society as a buffer to state power—a buffer which may be more effective than constitutionalism or constitutional engineering (which too often is hijacked by political elites). Returning to developments in Central and Eastern Europe, she notes the energies invested by many engaged intellectuals in an effort to theorize civil society "as an alternative to, or even in opposition to, an authoritarian sovereign state apparatus." Prominent among these intellectuals were Adam Michnik, who sought to hold "effective power and robust ethics" in fruitful tension with each other, and Václav Havel, who downplayed sovereignty "in favor of civil society as both a domestic and international imperative." For Elshtain, the civil-society perspective reveals the state as a public entity chiefly designed "to see that rules for civility are followed" and that the various "loci of human social existence," embedded in "mediating" institutions, are protected and served. Following Hedley Bull and others, Elshtain is willing to extend the nation of civil society to the global arena, which leads her to a "chastened" vision of sovereignty as an agency "protective of plurality internally and universal aspirations externally" and hence of a global village where states are "nested in wider societies, in strategic cultures." As one may note, this vision was not alien to Hegel, the great philosopher of mediation (too often accused of favoring inter-state rivalry). As Hegel observed in his *Philosophy of*

Right, the desire for sovereign autonomy among modern states is crisscrossed and counterbalanced by multiple forms of social and cultural interactions which, in the long run, may establish a common bond more effective than abstract imperatives. "International society," from this angle, appears as the fruit of a learning process whereby countries come to know and appreciate diverse cultural traditions, without erecting them into bastions of hostility.[9]

These mediating accents carry over from the theme of sovereignty into Elshtain's reflections on the "new nationalism," that is, on the upsurge of nationalist fervor and struggles for self-determination in many parts of the world. Quite often, this upsurge is bemoaned simply as a deplorable derailment, as an atavistic relapse contrary to the standards of enlightened modernity. In her lectures, Elshtain gives the example of Sir Julian Huxley who, a few decades ago, had predicted the demise of both nationalism and religion, viewing them purely as premodern relics destined to give way to the reign of "science and reason." As in the case of sovereignty, the situation for Elshtain is more complex and nuanced, requiring the exercise of careful, differentiated judgment. Although often derailing into chauvinism and xenophobia, nationalism—she recognizes—is also intricately linked with questions of self-identity, self-determination, and the maintenance of distinctive, historically sedimented life-forms. In this respect, she agrees with Liah Greenfeld's argument that national self-assertion is "a matter of dignity," a focal resource giving people "reasons to be proud." The same point was also made by Václav Havel when he depicted national independence movements as reflecting the "desire to renew and emphasize one's identity," in opposition to the "shroud of uniformity" imposed by global superpowers. Viewed from this angle, nationalism emerges as an ambivalent idea or political motivation. What is wrong in nationalism is not so much the loyalty or attachment to a distinctive life-form, but rather the excess of attachment—the perversion of loyalty into arrogant claims of superiority or into a fortified kind of particularism devoid of respect or concern for others.

The path preferred by Elshtain, in existential terms, is one steering clear both of spectatorial indifference and of hyper-involvement in concrete human affairs; transferred to the global arena, this path

shies away both from a bland cosmopolitanism—often a window-
dressing for hegemonic designs—and a militant "identity politics"
pitting nation against nation, culture against culture. Drawing on
papal encyclicals and other church documents, the Hesburgh Lectures counsel a *via media* or middle path, eloquently stated in these
terms: "a moderate but firm course between the Scylla of sovereign
absolutism, or an absolutizing of particular identities, and the
Charybdis of an arrogant universalism or imperialism running
roughshod over self-determination and diversity." In good Hegelian
(and perhaps Aristotelian) fashion, the middle path involves a mediation between universal and particular aspirations, between the
striving for reasonably "open borders" and the maintenance and cultivation of distinct life-forms. In Elshtain's words, the path consti-
tutes the only possible course that "respects claims to self-determination" while also keeping alive the prospect of a painfully attained
civic order based on "universal principles of recognition." Not un-
expectedly, the same path also carries Augustinian overtones, by
intimating the difficult relationship between "two cities" which,
though closely linked, cannot be fully merged. Pointing to the
fledgling patriotism of a South African theologian in the wake of
apartheid, Elshtain perceives in it an exemplary lesson: the lesson of
how people formed in the Christian tradition are "rightly drawn
toward the civic goods embodied in a particular order" but must at
the same time refuse any moves "to forge too tight an identity between their religious commitments and their national loyalties."

The *via media* of the Hesburgh Lectures also brings back into
view the complex correlation of ethics and (international) politics,
that is, their peculiarly differentiated entwinement. Given the situ-
atedness of human life-forms and the legitimacy of particular aspirations, politics for Elshtain cannot entirely be reduced to moralistic
principles or to a thin "blanket of ethical normativity." Particularly
in view of the vulnerability of the weak, politics cannot wholly be
severed from power. As she writes, following Hannah Arendt, resort
to power in politics is not necessarily an "ethical lapse," as it may
be undertaken "in the name of justice." Seen from this angle, ethics
in the political context cannot simply be equated with self-abandon-
ment or with a pliant surrender to heteronomy or "otherness" (a

position sometimes associated with the name of Emmanuel Levinas). Given the prevailing power differentials in the world, an ethics
of surrender too easily plays into the hands of ruling elites, by un-
dercutting or rendering suspect the stamina needed to resist oppres-
sion. On the other hand, politics, especially power politics, does not
hold the ultimate trump card over ethics. In Elshtain's words: "Not
power *über alles,* God forbid." Averse to pliant surrender, her *via
media* also rejects and condemns aggressive self-aggrandizement and
especially the equation of politics with conflict or the sheer struggle
for power. Rigorously applied, this equation involves the unmediated clash between self-enclosed identities, the contest between "us"
and "them," "friend" and "enemy"—congruent with Carl Schmitt's
definition of "the political." In light of the recent upsurge of
Schmitt's prestige in Western political thought, Elshtain's demurral
is sobering and refreshing. As she states (or perhaps understates) her
case in her lectures: "The presupposition of an enemy is not the
place from which one starts."[10]

As can readily be seen, the implications of Elshtain's *via media*
are multiple and far-reaching, although not all of them are spelled
out in her lectures. Regarding the notion of politics or "the political," her approach stands ajar both to a placid "meeting of minds"
and to a radical "agonistics"—especially an agonistics marked by a
total hiatus between contestants or by (what sometimes is called)
an "incommensurability of language games." This latter aspect helps
to profile and sharpen further Elshtain's view of the "limits" of
politics. As previously indicated, these limits for her are not merely
contingently imposed but rather are intrinsic constraints—a point
which puts her at odds with prominent, avant-gardist trends in contemporary political thought. Under the influence partly of Schmitt
and partly of "bold postmodern" thinkers, politics today is often
equated with strategic decision-making in the pursuit of power, a
pursuit which is in principle unbounded (and only factually bounded
by countervailing power). Although valuable as a corrective to a
"minimalist" politics (dear to liberal ideologues), this view tends to
privilege—perhaps rashly—political will-power over reason, parti-
san decisions over collaboration. Thus, relying on certain "decon-

structive" teachings, Ernesto Laclau at one point locates strategic decision "at the heart of any action which can be called political," adding that acts of political decision are not bounded but "self-grounding" in that they open up the possibility of conceiving "any political order as having a purely hegemonic and transient founda-tion."[11] Despite contingent qualifications (duly noted by Laclau), this conception rigorously pursued ultimately leads back to "incommensurability" and to the vision of politics as centered on "blind armies clashing at night."

Elshtain would hardly object to this vision as such—not in our bloody and war-torn century—only to its elevation to a general po-litical theory. Her lectures are packed with references to the im-mense agonies and atrocities of our age: from Auschwitz and Bosnia to Rwanda and Northern Ireland. Yet, it is precisely in these accounts that her ethical sensibilities surface, by registering a profound out-rage rooted in the complicity with history's victims. Without offer-ing, or even flirting with, grand utopian panaceas, her lectures re-sound with the grief of the afflicted and oppressed—a grief which, better than abstract imperatives, pronounces an indictment of bloodthirst and violence as intolerable assaults on the "human con-dition." Thus, ethical sensibility, without domineering gesture, in-habits or slumbers in the heart of politics, even the politics of our violent century. This is what leads Elshtain, in her concluding epi-logue, to ponder the meaning of one of the key terms in Arendt's vocabulary: that of "forgiveness." Although there surely are "no sac-raments" or "benedictions" in ordinary politics, there still is an ur-gent human need to step back from hurt and injury to make room for something distantly approximating a "redemption narrative," in order "to forestall quaffing the bitter brew of injustice suffered and recompense sought even unto future generations." Perhaps recon-ciliation would be a better term than forgiveness, because, as Elshtain observes, forgiving here cannot be a "one-way street" but implies a relationship or "transitive dimension" (an aspect which seems better captured in the former term). The idea of reconcili-ation as an overcoming of enmity or "diremption" is one of the deepest strands in the philosophy of Hegel, who not by accident has been called *the* philosopher of reconciliation. As one should note, reconciliation for Hegel (as for Elshtain) is not an external limit but pervades political practice itself—in fact, it is at work in the midst of political violence or war. Here is what we read in the *Philosophy of Right:*

> By virtue of the mutual recognition among states, there remains even in war—that condition of lawlessness, brute force, and accident—a bond whereby states count as autonomously existing for each other (or in reciprocity). Hence in the midst of armed conflict, war itself is marked as something transitory which ought to cease. This implies the provision of the *jus gentium* that warfare should preserve the possible restoration of peace.[12]

Hegel's philosophy of reconciliation resonates on the religious plane with the message of Christianity, which is a message of (divine-human and inter-human) reconciliation. Quite appropriately, the theme of reconciliation and mediation loomed large in the work of St. Augustine, for whom all forms of life, from the lowest to the highest, were geared toward the goal of peace. This point is recognized in the *Augustine* study when Elshtain writes that, for the bishop, "the end game is not talk of power, or sovereignty, or national interest, but only of peace. From the tigress purring over her cubs, to human fellowship in all its forms, peace, even a pale peace unworthy of the name, is the ultimate aim of conflict." She quotes Augustine himself to the effect that "peace is the instinctive aim of all creatures, and is even the ultimate purpose of war," and comments: "Oddly enough, when people fight it is to draw fighting to a close." As one might add, the striving for peace and reconciliation is hardly a uniquely or exclusively Christian quality, but is shared by all or most of the world's great religions. The emphasis in Buddhism on nonviolence and nonaggression is widely known and rightly praised. Drawing on a welter of Buddhist, Jain, and Hindu teachings, Mahatma Gandhi made nonviolence or *ahimsa* a cornerstone of his struggle for Indian independence, thereby infusing a glimmer of light into an otherwise dark and violence-ridden era. Even Islam—a religion often denounced (in the West) as violence-prone—

is basically oriented toward peace (which is the meaning of the Arabic root *silm* in Islam.) Pointing to such Quranic verses as "reconciliation is the best" and "God calls to the home of peace," a contemporary Muslim leader affirms eloquently that "Islam enjoins us to establish peace even at the cost of unilateral sacrifice and patience"; it aims "at making all individuals peace-loving to the ultimate extent. That is why we are enjoined to greet one another by saying *Assalam-o-Aleikum,* that is, peace be upon you."[13]

As it happens—surprisingly, perhaps, in our somber times—longing for peace and forgiveness are not entirely left on the plane of pious sentiments, but are translated at least occasionally into political practice. In the case of the Sudetenland mentioned in Elshtain's epilogue, the two parties to the dispute, Germany and the Czech Republic, have signed an official "Declaration of Reconciliation" (January 1997), culminating two years of negotiations. As the German chancellor observed at the signing ceremony, the declaration represented a step toward "breaking the vicious circle of mutual recriminations," thus liberating both parties from being "prisoners of the past."[14] Similar efforts at peace-making and forgiving—not in the sense of a simple forgetting, but also of rectifying past injustices—have been and are underway in other parts of the world, including Central America and Africa. Thus, in Panama a Commission of Justice and Peace has been trying to heal the wounds stemming from abuses of the previous Noriega regime. In South Africa, Mandela, soon after taking office, established a Truth and Reconciliation Commission charged with the task of both providing a public record of, and finding reconciling ways to redress, past injustices and acts of violence. A difficult case is presented by Northern Ireland, where the prospects of peace and reconciliation still seem distant and elusive. In a way, the poignancy of the case is increased by the locale of the Hesburgh Lectures. Elshtain points to the stirring call for *metanoia* issued by the Catholic Cardinal of Northern Ireland and also to the corresponding sentiments expressed by the Archbishop of Canterbury. However, the question remains whether reconciling efforts can be left to church leaders alone. Should a certain share of moral responsibility not also rest on

the shoulders of a university which is nationally and even internationally known for a team called "The Fighting Irish"? Should such
a university not more vocally enter the peace process: by insisting
that "fighting" be left to the sports field while wanton acts of violence and destruction are condemned?

Before concluding, it may be proper for me to raise a few queries
or afterthoughts, not for the sake of instant settlement, but rather
for future discussion. One point which leaves me uneasy in her lectures is Elshtain's treatment of "multiculturalism," which, in her
presentation, seems to coincide with fragmentation or (what she
calls) an "absolutism of particular identities." As it appears to me,
despite certain "bold postmodern" leanings in that direction, fragmentation does not capture the nuanced multiculturalism of writers
like Charles Taylor or Michael Walzer (whose views actually seem
close to her own "civic pluralism").[15] Another point deserving in-
quiry is Elshtain's complex relationship with Hannah Arendt, one
of her chosen mentors with whom, as the lectures show, she remains
closely yet critically engaged. An intriguing element in this relation
is the figure of St. Augustine—from whom Arendt's work took its
initial departure, while Elshtain has been steadily moving toward
him ("on the footpath that leads away from Wittenberg" in a south-
erly direction). A further issue might be of a more theological nature, involving the effect of the twilight of political sovereignty on
its theistic model, that is, on the *imago Dei* (in its post-Occamite as
well as its trinitarian form). However, rather than pursuing these
questions, I want to close by returning to the practical import of
Elshtain's lectures—at century's end and at millennium's end. This
impact is eloquently expressed in her *Augustine* book, in a plea
which is urgent yet without false utopianism:

> The *saeculum* is the here and now. It is in the here and now that
> war and peace get played out. If the Christian is a disturber of a
> false peace, he or she yearns for a more authentic representation of
> earthly peace as that which partakes in the *pax aeterna*. . . . The
> Christian caught in temporality is pressed by "the selfsame press
> as the bad." The press is Augustine's analogy to an olive press,
> squeezing olives for oil. Thus we are pressed. But our life of fel-

lowship—a *vita socialis sanctorum*—calls us, not to perfection, but to relative peace. The Heavenly City is a perfect vision of peace. But there is earthly work to be done in the name of peace.[16]

NOTES

1. Jean Bethke Elshtain, *Augustine and the Limits of Politics* (Notre Dame, Ind.: University of Notre Dame Press, 1995), p. III.
2. *Augustine and the Limits of Politics,* pp. 51–52.
3. *Augustine and the Limits of Politics,* p. 15. The earlier reference is to Fredric Jameson, *The Prison-House of Language* (Princeton, N.J.: Princeton University Press, 1972).
4. Elshtain, *Augustine and the Limits of Politics,* pp. xi–xii, 69–71. As Elshtain reminds her readers, Camus himself had written a dissertation on St. Augustine and Neoplatonism.
5. Elshtain, *Democracy on Trial* (New York: Basic Books, 1993), pp. 42–45. As she adds in the same study, critiquing what she calls the "politics of displacement" (p. 40): "If all conceptual boundaries are blurred and all distinctions between public and private eliminated, no politics can exist, by definition. By *politics,* I refer to that which is, in principle, held in common and what is, in principle, open to public scrutiny and judgment." Compare also Elshtain, *Public Man, Private Woman: Women in Social and Political Thought* (Princeton, N.J.: Princeton University Press, 1981).
6. See Hannah Arendt, *The Human Condition: A Study of the Central Dilemmas Facing Modern Man* (Garden City, N.Y.: Doubleday Anchor Books, 1958), and *The Origins of Totalitarianism* (New York: Harcourt, Brace and World, 1951).
7. Arendt, "What is Freedom?" in *Between Past and Future* (New York: Penguin Books, 1980), pp. 164–165.
8. Dr. Chandra Muzaffer, "Anwar and Future Challenges," in *Just Commentary* 36 (January 1997), p. 11. As one should note, fortifying indigenous culture for Muzaffer is far removed from any self-enclosed fundamentalism. On the contrary, fortifying culture means precisely to retrieve and revive "the universal" in local traditions. This goal is buttressed by cross-cultural dialogue, seeking to develop a "deeper and better understanding between and among cultures and civilizations."
9. G. W. F. Hegel, *Grundlinien der Philosophie des Rechts* (Frankfurt: Suhrkamp, 1976), par. 339, pp. 502–503; *Hegel's Philosophy of Right,* trans.

T. M. Knox (Oxford: Oxford University Press, 1967), pp. 215, 297. See also my *G. W. F. Hegel: Modernity and Politics* (Newbury Park, Calif.: Sage Publications, 1993), pp. 158–159.

10. Regarding a "heteronomous" ethics, see Emmanuel Levinas, *Totality and Infinity: An Essay on Exteriority*, trans. Alphonso Lingis (Pittsburgh, Penn.: Duquesne University Press, n.d.), pp. 33–52, 194–219. Regarding the friend-enemy conception, see Carl Schmitt, *The Concept of the Political*, trans. George Schwab (New Brunswick, N.J.: Rutgers University Press, 1976). As an antidote to a bland consensualism, Schmitt's conception is invoked today even by very nuanced democratic thinkers, e.g., by Chantal Mouffe in her *The Return of the Political* (London: Verso, 1993). Yet, although repeatedly citing the "friend / enemy" formula, Mouffe qualifies her endorsement in these terms (p. 4): "Once we accept the necessity of the political and the impossibility of a world without antagonism, what needs to be envisaged is how it is possible *under those conditions* to create or maintain a pluralistic democratic order. Such an order is based on a distinction between 'enemy' and 'adversary'."

11. Ernesto Laclau, "Deconstruction, Pragmatism, Hegemony," in Chantal Mouffe, ed., *Deconstruction and Pragmatism* (London and New York: Routledge, 1996), p. 66. Laclau explicitly refers to Derridean deconstruction (pp. 52–53), noting that, because in deconstructive analysis "structure is undecidable," political decision "cannot be ultimately grounded in anything external to itself." He also quotes Derrida himself to the effect: "The instance of the decision is madness, says Kierkegaard." For the latter statement, see Jacques Derrida, "Force of Law: The 'Mystical Foundation of Authority'," in Drucilla Cornell, Michael Rosenfeld, and David G. Carlson, eds., *Deconstruction and the Possibility of Justice* (London and New York: Routledge, 1992), p. 26.

12. Hegel, *Grundlinien der Philosophie des Rechts*, par. 338, p. 502; *Hegel's Philosophy of Right*, p. 215. For the portrayal of Hegel as philosopher of reconciliation, see Hans-Georg Gadamer, *Reason in the Age of Science*, trans. Frederick G. Lawrence (Cambridge, Mass.: MIT Press, 1981), pp. 27–29, 34–35. Compare also Gregory Baum and Harold Wells, eds., *The Reconciliation of Peoples: Challenge to the Churches* (Maryknoll, N.Y.: Orbis Books, 1997); and my "Critical Theory and Reconciliation," in Dallmayr, *Between Freiburg and Frankfurt: Toward a Critical Ontology* (Amherst: University of Massachusetts Press, 1991), pp. 72–104.

13. Maulana Wahiduddin Khan, "Islam and Peace," in *Al-Risala* 129 (March–April 1996), pp. 3–5. See also Elshtain, *Augustine and the Limits of Politics*, pp. 108–109. The earlier quotation is from Augustine's *De civitate Dei*, Book 19, chapter 12.

14. "Fact Sheet," *German Information Center*, January 1997, p. 1.

15. Compare Amy Gutmann, ed., *Multiculturalism: Examining the Politics of Recognition* (Princeton, N.J.: Princeton University Press, 1994). The book contains a major essay by Charles Taylor and commentaries by Anthony Appiah, Jürgen Habermas, Steven C. Rockefeller, Michael Walzer, and Susan Wolf. See also my "Democracy and Multiculturalism," in Dallmayr, *Beyond Orientalism: Essays on Cross-Cultural Encounter* (Albany, N.Y.: SUNY Press, 1996), pp. 201–222.

16. Elshtain, *Augustine and the Limits of Politics*, pp. xiii, 105.

FORGIVENESS, DESPITE THE PRESSURES OF SOVEREIGNTY AND NATIONALISM

Martha Merritt

JEAN BETHKE ELSHTAIN apprehends politics and ethics in ways that encourage our perception and celebration of their intersection. Her work also features an awareness of less heartening possibilities concerning the exercise of political power. The conceptual richness of these lectures and the texture of her vocabulary make it a pleasure to comment upon the important themes of sovereignty, nationalism, and forgiveness. This essay serves to underscore the linkages among these issues and also to consider how the all-important process of reconciliation, which Elshtain invokes to challenge the temptation of blood feud, may be facilitated.

One political struggle that animates sovereignty struggles is the search for a common basis of membership that leaders can utilize and followers find convincing. We perhaps underestimate the difficulty of securing sovereignty and defining membership in a way that will make sense to its constituents and remain morally acceptable to those outside the community. The seeking of a master narrative to represent a unified will is not, it seems to me, merely an obsession on the part of nationalistic politicians and scholars, but rather the quest of human beings as we order our house, our community, our political universe.

Loss of opposition to the Soviet Union as an organizing principle has been a serious blow for democratic countries and their ability to link morality with foreign policy. This linkage, distressingly rare, was also not very convincing when anti-communism was the only moral touchstone. Intellectual power has suffered as well: we seem to have little conceptual role for politics in this new world order other than its role in allowing markets to deal with other markets. Both the ways in which changing political systems can be identified and the criteria by which democracy can be understood are obscured when we assume that those viewing democracy simply as the means to prosperity can build liberal democracy. Categorizing societies and governments as "transitional" is often an attempt to see universalism pending where dissonance exists.

The phenomenon called globalism presents many challenges for analysis, not the least of which is determining what globalism signifies. What would an increase or decrease of it look like? The tendency among scholars is to measure the progress of globalism vis-à-vis the demise of the state. Although this process is generally considered to be a zero-sum game, it carries no clear picture of an end result: what seems to be meant is movement toward a world in which communication and trade face fewer obstacles in the form of state boundaries. In this light, globalism is portrayed not just as the beneficiary of the demise of the state, but as an important contributing factor. And few who write about globalism express regret over the state's presumed decline.

One of the reasons for globalism's favorable press is a sense that the European model of modern state has committed crimes for which little accountability and few policing mechanisms have been instituted. Lack of trust in the voracious state gives rise to sentiments such as David Held's, that "national democracies require international democracy if they are to be sustained and developed in the contemporary world."[1] Measures thought to improve accountability of government—including education of the public in order to promote deliberative democracy, direct vote via propositions and other citizen referenda, and transparency of the political process—have gained popularity as solutions to what is widely seen as a dilemma of democratic government concerning accountability.

Part of the problem may be the necessity, as Dankwart Rustow pointed out in 1970, of settling the national and state question prior to working on further refinements like democracy.[2] The bloody years since the end of the Cold War have raised the question of whether many states are secure within their boundaries, and this language is to be taken literally: the security of state structures and not the state as shorthand for the people who live under its jurisdiction. If states became significantly weaker, would we then have a better world and hope of a settled political order? When a well-established democracy like Canada faces questions of secession and indigenous land rights that would severely tax any political institution, democratic or otherwise, the past injustices of the state must be considered as well as the uncertainty that redistribution of power can curtail future abuse.

I would like to focus on the challenge of ethnic political identity and the state as it pertains to the notion of sovereignty in Elshtain's essays. The vocabulary of ethnic identity can reveal or recast the state as empire. The emergence of ethnically based nation-states, greatly increased with the collapse of the Soviet Union, pinpoints this trend: minority constituencies who portray their own national community as finite, special, and different often want these differences to merit new state boundaries. The nation, a human community, is seen as stifled by and vulnerable to suppression in a multinational state. As separatist or secessionist movements grow, the state becomes increasingly blurred with empire in the rhetoric of the minority. Few would contest this interpretation in the case of the Soviet bloc; less remarked upon is the similarity between the rhetoric of, say, the Estonian and the Québécois independence movements. Invoking the umbrella state as empire is part of the sovereignty struggle that characterizes what Elshtain and others call the new nationalism.

One of the justifications for sovereignty is a state defined by ethnicity, however unrealistic that goal may prove. How are we to understand the role of publics in these ethnically-defined states? This question begs the thorny issue of how we understand the "new" nationalism. What exactly was the "old" nationalism?

Some scholars see nationalism, writ favorably, as based on the European nineteenth-century model of civic nationalism that leans toward inclusion (sometimes forcible inclusion) and then leaves space for creation and recreation. Contemporary scholars who live under civic nationalism tend to subscribe to the separation of civic from ethnic nationalism, the former inclusionary and desirable, the latter separatist and intolerant. Yet the stresses and strains within the civic nationalist model, in some states listing toward constitutional revision, would suggest that all is not well with the European model either. Elshtain contrasts a sort of watery universalism with a rapacious nationalism.

I wonder if in fact we might better understand nationalism if we interpret the watery universalism not only as empire, an obvious negative, but very likely as a minority group's interpretation of civic nationalism. The rhetoric of a sovereignty movement within an "old," albeit derivative, nationalist framework can be cast as the "new" nationalism—or perhaps as the long-delayed reaction to the "old" nationalism, which wrought its own wrongs in the struggle for sovereignty.

How, then, are we to understand Eric Hobsbawm's contention that nationalism, rather than being resurgent, is in fact a dying phenomenon?[3] By severely limiting the cases referred to as exercises of nationalism, Hobsbawm is able to maintain a sense of nationalism as a positive force, giving way to divisive and negative forces in the twentieth century. This is a great leap from nationalism as understood by Elie Kedourie, for example, who considered it a consistently violent and unpleasant modern phenomenon, whether in this century or the last. In this sense, Kedourie's major book on nationalism,[4] first published in 1960 and in its fourth edition in 1993, seems readily applicable to the post-Soviet states; Hobsbawm sidesteps the linkage by implying that we are dealing with a more primitive force, better categorized as ethnicity, that seeks to destroy what nationalism created.

It is worthwhile at this point to probe Hobsbawm's interpretation of contemporary ethnic movements. The first edition of *Nations and Nationalism since 1780,* published in 1990, has a revealing concluding chapter. Some of the changes between this conclusion and Hobsbawm's revised conclusion for the second edition in 1992 illustrate his distinctive view.

In 1990, Hobsbawm defines contemporary nationalism as modern ethnic struggle involving "reactions of weakness and fear." This is not true nationalism because the cry for national state has become so ubiquitous as to render it meaningless; much of this movement is better understood as political paranoia (such as the movement in the United States to make English the official language). According to this version of Hobsbawm's conclusion, even national states under significant assault could scarcely be said to struggle against the same force that forged national states in Europe in the last century. Modern claims for self-determination are "rejections of modern modes of political organization, both national and supranational." Finally, in a world of bipolar power relations and the resulting two broad alliances, states and the forces which bind them play a less important role.

Hobsbawm's attempt to portray modern self-determination as regressive and thus a rejection of both national and supranational organizations has not been borne out by what he might call "ethnic experience" in the 1990s. New or reestablished states in eastern Europe, for example, are for the most part desperate for membership in supranational organizations such as NATO and the European Union. Likewise, the breakdown of global bipolarity could be said to have reasserted nationalism as a contemporary force. Hobsbawm nevertheless went back into his text not to change his conclusions, but to tinker with the explanatory factors leading to them.

In 1992 we read that nationalism is no longer a vector of historical change. Contemporary nationalism has no national goal beyond separation from larger-scale authority, thus marking it as distinct from last century's version. Here it is tempting to bring back Kedourie, for whom today's conflicts would represent the fallout of the earlier, equally "artificial" concept of nationalism in the last major round of European state formation. John Breuilly has always interpreted nationalism as an instrumental rallying cry representing the needs of a parasitic creature, dependent upon and shaped by what it opposes.[5] Thus, nationalism can be unifying when it confronts fragmenting political systems or separatist when it confronts that which has been united. Hobsbawm's otherwise compelling portrait of modern European state-building becomes less convincing as he takes on the forces influencing contemporary states. It is difficult to see how current ethnic mobilization could *not* have been shaped by state structures and *not* draw support from contemporary superstructure, in particular the global community.

What does a world with increasing numbers of ethnically defined states look like? Ethnocracies hovering on the borders of conventional states represent relatively unstable political systems, based, as they are, on protest mobilization against a more powerful authority. If a state increasingly cast as empire by dissatisfied minority groups wants to enhance its standing, one can imagine a scenario under which territory is reconceptualized in order to emphasize the broad nation over the misbehaving smaller one: military questions at least remain centered on the state. This is not to suggest that Canada is going to pounce on Manhattan in order to silence Quebec. A more likely scenario is that the establishment of an ethnocracy, rather than the mere threat of it, destabilizes the state from which it seceded, bringing a situation of frail new state and ailing neighboring state.

Some of the purposes of the European model state which are distinctive from ethnocracy's status as bearer of national identity, or empire's as guarantor of order, are management of fiscal policy and the bearing of blame. The bearing of blame in particular presents a paradox: the more the state takes on without being able to defend itself convincingly, the more likely that dissatisfied groups in society can articulate their demands in ways which aim to weaken further the state. Some minority groups are finding that the state is more their protector than their enemy as membership is redefined.

Sadly, there is no guarantee that accountability will be improved if power flows to local authority and / or supranational authority. This comment, stimulated by Elshtain's linkage of sovereignty and nationalism, suggests that relying on regional and global arrangements may actually lessen the responsibility of political actors, particularly given their acquisition of power in an anti-state climate. The service rendered by many new regimes is elimination of the old regime, not necessarily improvement of the mechanisms which brought about dissatisfaction in the first place (especially official corruption). The way this blaming and re-formation plays out depends in part on what kind of state was present. Much of the writing on globalism can thus be described as a celebration of human potential, without yet offering many guidelines in assessing the gritty realities of state breakdown.

In an attempt to tie together the three themes running through this essay, and far more profoundly, through Elshtain's lectures, let us consider the following question: How can sovereign states facilitate a climate of forgiveness? I understand forgiveness as a sort of release, and not the only kind of release possible for an aggrieved party. Reconciliation also includes the possibility of blame, for wrong has been done, but the wrong is rectified only through morally acceptable means. Some of the great universalist writers such as Václav Havel, whose powerful message Elshtain invokes, recommend forgiveness but also chronicle wrongdoing. And how else are we to understand the great Russian poet Anna Akhmatova's *Requiem,* her homage to those who suffered under Stalinism, except as a reconciliation to a pain so vast that not addressing it means condoning inhumanity?

Akhmatova spent seventeen months waiting to discover the fate of her son, who had been arrested in order to silence the powerful poet and mother. In *Requiem* the poet speaks of a woman, lips blue from the cold, who approaches her after many days of waiting together. The woman has woken up to the possibility of justice, not from murderous officials, but from a famous writer. Her request is simple:

'Can you describe this?'
And I answered, 'Yes, I can.'
Then something like a smile passed over what had once been her face.[6]

What is this woman smiling about? Surely it is not a vengeful smile on that ravaged visage. The woman has a flash of life left in her which wants to know that all their suffering was not in vain, all will not be forgotten and their lives misplaced: Akhmatova can leave a record. This record is unlikely to be used to bring the individuals who wronged them to trial, and indeed their names are not known. The value of the record is its role in asserting human dignity under awesome cruelty, perhaps even to prevent a duplication of this particular man-made horror.

Thus, one condition that facilitates forgiveness is the presence of gifted writers or leaders, an Akhmatova, a Havel, a Mandela, who by their grace and presence demonstrate their own reconciliation with hard fate and allow the rest of us to find forgiveness in our hearts. But these humanist writers and leaders are rare. And a necessary condition for their message to reach us is a regime willing to facilitate reconciliation or at least unable to halt the process of truth telling. Spiritual leaders often urge the state to accept accountability for its actions. Such an admission of responsibility skates the fine line between responsibility and guilt, and carries with it the risk of subsequent demand for recompense, ranging from restitution of property to the falling of a regime. The stakes for both sides in such a conflict are significant and involve much jockeying to define the moral high ground.

Having considered the nobility of those who could easily seek revenge but find it unacceptable, we should explore the motivation of less famous folk who also made sacrifices difficult to comprehend in comfortable western societies. During the last ten years, thousands of people in Eurasia traveled many miles and endured many benches in order to clear the names of their relatives besmirched during the Stalin years. In some cases these were relatives they had never met or even relatives they did not know of until recently. Some also went to discover the facts of their past in newly opened archives in Russia and eastern Europe. For scholars it is an incredible and profound experience to sift through long-hidden secrets come to light. But how much more intense the experiences of those around us in the archives, who are there to discover the fate of lost relatives and friends. A woman cries softly, and then passes around a picture she has found. She is not in the archive to find those who killed him, or necessarily to record anything from the file (unlike the scholars laboring around her). It is as if she needed to see the written records and the photograph to erase the lines on her forehead, the pain in her heart, the hatred in her soul. Thus is cleared the space for positive construction, of personal identity, of nation, of state.

States have an obligation to facilitate forgiveness by addressing their current or previous crimes, and so to the example mentioned by Elshtain of the Sudetenland Germans and a need to let go of the past. This is morally desirable, but I am not sure that people find their way to forgiveness unacknowledged, unescorted. And unfortunately, wrongs which go unrectified often do so because current beliefs still harbor prejudice and vengeful discrimination. The recommendation to let go of old wrongs is often addressed to the weaker of the two constituencies, the non-state or non-majority party that needs to stop making a fuss and let life go on.

Václav Havel opposed most of his Czech compatriots when he extended words of sorrow to the Sudetenland Germans in 1990. The reconciliation that Havel instigated was not made official until seven years later, and then to the consternation of many on both sides. Sudetenland Germans feared they were being cheated by their own government out of restitution for historical wrongs, and from the Czech side, officials were sufficiently wary of public reaction to postpone agreement on the official apology until after parliamentary elections. The Czech public might not forgive the official apologists, and thus the difference between an apology from a government and genuine repentance from a public needs to be emphasized. Poles in Lithuania today, Russians in Estonia and Latvia, experience not violations of human rights but razor-sharp flicks of petty bureaucratic tyranny. And most maddening to these groups is the knowledge that this is all part of the exercise of sovereignty and, once the rules of the game are codified, is relatively impervious to the influence of international organizations.

Those who would hold states accountable sometimes have trouble "perceiving" them from within. Some then apprehend the state as "other" and are likely to resort to nationalism to regain perspective on what comes to seem a smothering dominant civic culture. Others choose to remain within the bounds of sovereignty but use the concept of revenge to make up for past wrongs. My remarks here no doubt illustrate the complexity of the moral political universe introduced by Elshtain, but I hope also underscore the worthiness of attempting to navigate it. Only by assuming political and ethical intersection can we know political discourse to be meaningful rather than arbitrary, and political power struggles to be as much about human needs as they are about human shortcomings. Forgiveness rests on those who apprehend regimes as both linked with their publics and subject to full accounting, but who know that each person from that state is not a miniature version of it. Those few who conduct the chronicle of wrongdoing with grace and mercy are all the more precious.

NOTES

1. David Held, "From City-States to a Cosmopolitan Order?" in David Held, ed., *Prospects for Democracy: North, South, East, West* (Cambridge: Polity Press, 1993), p. 14.

2. Dankwart Rustow, "Transitions to Democracy: Towards a Dynamic Model," *Comparative Politics* 2 (April 1970), pp. 337–363.

3. Under discussion here is E. J. Hobsbawm, *Nations and Nationalism since 1780* (Cambridge: Cambridge University Press), both the 1990 version and the conclusion of the revised 1992 edition.

4. Elie Kedourie, *Nationalism*, 4th ed. (Oxford: Blackwell, 1993).

5. John Breuilly, *Nationalism and the State*, 2d ed. (Chicago: University of Chicago Press, 1993).

6. This excerpt from *Requiem* was translated by the author. For a complete translation of the poem, see Judith Hemschemeyer, trans. *The Complete Poems of Anna Akhmatova* (Boston: Zephyr Press, 1983), pp. 384–394.